# A PRACTICAL GUIDE TO FINDING YOUR SPIRITUAL GIFTS

TYNDALE HOUSE
PUBLISHERS, INC.
WHEATON, ILLINOIS

# TIM
# BLANCHARD

A
PRACTICAL
GUIDE TO

# Finding
# Your
# Spiritual
# Gifts

Library of Congress
Catalog Card Number 78-66199.
ISBN 0-8423-4877-8,
paper.
Copyright © 1979
by Tim Blanchard.
All rights reserved.
First printing, July 1979.
Printed in
the United States of America.

*To my wife, Barbara,*
*who has consistently*
*demonstrated to me*
*the greatest spiritual gift,*
*love.*

# CONTENTS

# PREFACE

I received my seminary training and began my pastoral ministry during the late 1960s and early 1970s at the height of the evangelical interest in spiritual gifts.

Upon entering my first pastorate, I searched for practical helps to guide our people in determining their spiritual gifts. I did not find in any one book or resource the material I believed was needed. As a result, God led and the Holy Spirit enabled me to forge out this manual.

I acknowledge particularly the helpful background materials developed by my good friends in the ministry: Stu Weber, John Peterson, and Galen Currah. Tapes and seminar materials of Dr. Earl Radmacher, Dr. Gordon McMinn, Dr. Ray Stedman, and Mr. Bill Gothard were also very helpful.

Loren Fischer of Western Conservative Baptist Seminary and Harold Westing of Conservative Baptist Seminary gave essential suggestions and critiques. Without their work, the manual would never have reached this stage of development and completion.

On a very practical level, I owe a great deal to my mother, Mrs. Lillian Blanchard, who spent many hours editing and typing. Finally, I was continually encouraged by the people of West Side Baptist Church, and their interest in finding and using their spiritual gifts. They, especially, have made this project worth the effort.

# INTRODUCTION

Christians have been talking much about spiritual gifts. But the discussions and debates have focused almost totally on what the gifts are, and which of the gifts are for today's church. This is unfortunate. Spiritual gifts should be viewed like any other gifts; the emphasis should be on *using and enjoying* them.

The Scriptures teach that Christians should fit into a spiritual body (the local church), just as physical members unite together in a physical body. One's spiritual gift gives him insight as to where and how he is to serve the church. This spiritual body needs the equivalent of hands, feet, eyes, joints, veins, and all the other bodily parts. The challenge is to find the right place and become useful in the body.

On the date of our spiritual birth, we receive our spiritual gift. However, we have no innate understanding of what it is or the fact that we have it. We must be taught. We are like the boy who, immediately after he was born, became heir to a fortune. The fortune took on meaning to him only when he learned that he was an heir with vast resources at his disposal.

Every thinking, full-time church worker knows that many ministries lie untouched because of the inactivity of some Christians. He also sees that the uninvolved do not move to maturity as quickly as those who are happily serving. How can these gifted but idle people be rallied to serve? Each must know his or her gift, and each must be properly motivated to rise up and meet a need.

For years, pastors and Christian leaders have encouraged workers to "get involved"—with only a fair degree of success. "Won't you give prayerful consideration to these needs that we have placed before you today?" Such pleas have abounded. Emphasis has been placed on recruiting techniques, spiritual arm-twisting, and emotional appeals. With these methods, one wonders how many parts of the spiritual body have been doing tasks designed for *other* parts to do.

Psychologist Leo MacManus declares that motivation comes alive when a person: a) gains recognition by others,

b) enjoys a sense of accomplishment, c) is impressed with the importance of the task he is doing, and d) holds a definite responsibility. Uninvolved people experience none of these motivators. They must take hold of the most exciting catalyst for involvement—spiritual gifts.

Every inactive member must be informed that he has a special, spiritual, God-given gift. When he sees that his gift is essential for the proper functioning of the church, the member immediately begins to feel biblically based recognition. Upon discovering his gift, his spiritual self-worth increases greatly. Training then builds confidence. Finally, he begins shouldering responsibilities and becomes increasingly inspired by a sense of personal accomplishment through doing an important task. A believer who properly understands and uses his spiritual gift becomes an enthusiastic worker.

This manual is a learning tool. It is intended to direct you, a gifted believer, on a course toward finding, understanding, and using your spiritual gift. The impact can be revolutionary. Why? Because spiritual gifts are God's way of equipping his believers to minister in his church. All other methods are inferior.

Paul charged the Corinthians, "Now, concerning spiritual gifts, brethren, I would not have you ignorant" (1 Corinthians 12:1). We must be faithful leaders and workers who heed this mandate.

(For those who would like to use these studies for a spiritual gifts seminar or as a Sunday school class quarter study, see Appendixes I and II, which discuss how to plan and structure such group studies.)

# ONE
# Distinguishing
# Some Terms

NATURAL TALENTS. Natural talents are inherited abilities and interests received at birth. "He's a natural athlete," says a proud mother, "just like his dad." Such talents become more obvious through education, training, and practice. Spiritual life is not necessary for their development.

These inborn abilities are often used in church work by dedicated Christians. However, they must be clearly distinguished from spiritual gifts. A Christian's spiritual gift may appear similar to one of his talents. However, the inner motivation will be different. And the degree and quality of effectiveness will also be different.

From the following biblical examples, write down the name of the person and his natural talent.

|  | Name | Natural talent |
|---|---|---|
| Genesis 4:2 | | |
| Genesis 4:20 | | |
| Genesis 4:21 | | |
| Genesis 4:22 | | |
| Genesis 25:27 | | |

NORMAL SPIRIT-CONTROLLED BEHAVIOR. When a person accepts the Lord Jesus Christ as his personal Savior, ". . . he is a new creature: old things are passed away; behold, all things are become new" (2 Corinthians 5:17). This new life is possible because the Holy Spirit of God indwells him (1 Corinthians 6:19). He has the responsibility to learn and obey the Scriptures, confess all known sin, and let the Spirit of God control his life. In so doing, his heart and soul, including natural talents, become a channel through which the Spirit can work.

The resulting Spirit-controlled attitudes and actions of the believer, such as love, joy, temperance, witnessing, giving, and exercising faith, are spiritual fruit. All Christians can and should bear these fruits—reveal these qualities—regardless of temperament, abilities, or spiritual gifts.

13

From the following verses, note the ways the Spirit-controlled life will be demonstrated.

1 Thessalonians 5:11_____
Galatians 5:13_____
Hebrews 10:25_____
2 Corinthians 9:7_____
2 Corinthians 5:7_____
1 John 4:1_____

Is it enough to be a Spirit-filled Christian who uses his natural talents for the Lord? No! There is more to the Christian life.

SPIRITUAL GIFTS. A spiritual gift is a supernatural gift of grace which is measured and given out by God to each true Christian as a stewardship for serving the church of Jesus Christ. Just as we receive our natural talents at the time of our first birth, so we receive our spiritual gift at the time of our second birth into spiritual life (1 Peter 4:10). Each gift is in the form of a specific spiritual ability for service. With it, the believer is to help build up the church and honor God. To be all that God desires, a Christian must know and use his spiritual gift.

This gift may, in certain cases, seem similar to our natural talents. It may also appear to be just the natural outcome of Spirit-controlled behavior. However, the Scriptures clearly label a spiritual gift as a distinct, special present from the Holy Spirit. We must realize that effective service in the church depends upon the proper understanding and use of our spiritual gift.

In the New Testament, two Greek words are translated "spiritual gifts." One is *neumatika* (1 Corinthians 12:1), from *neuma*, meaning "breath or spirit." This term emphasizes the inner spiritual motivation that comes with the gift.

The other word is *charismata* (Romans 12:6), from *charis*, meaning grace. This term emphasizes God's grace (unmerited love of God to man) in outward display. By grace, the gifted believer is capable of demonstrating spiritual ability in the church, where all can see. It is God who provides both the inner motivation for, and the outward expression of, a person's spiritual gift.

Prior to Pentecost, the Spirit of God indwelt God-fearing

14

believers only in certain instances. He was more normally "upon" them (Numbers 11:17), and "among" them (Haggai 2:5). However, the Spirit did enter mightily into some select Old Testament servants, indwelling, filling, and gifting them for service by a single divine act. Indicate below the names of six such persons and the type of spiritual gift each received.

|  | *Name* | *Gift* |
|---|---|---|
| Genesis 41:38 | | |
| Exodus 31:3, 6 | | |
| Numbers 11:25, 26 | | |
| Numbers 27:18-20 | | |
| Deuteronomy 34:9 | | |
| Daniel 4:8b, 18 | | |

These occasions of indwelling and gifting seem to be forerunners of the Church Age. Today, in the Church Age, all believers are indwelt by the Spirit, and all are gifted for service.

Three main lists of spiritual gifts are recorded in the New Testament. From the Scripture verses below, list the gifts you see in these key passages:

*Romans 12:6-8*

1. _____
2. _____
3. _____
4. _____
5. _____
6. _____
7. _____

*1 Corinthians 12:8-10*

1. _____
2. _____
3. _____
4. _____
5. _____
6. _____
7. _____
8. _____
9. _____

*1 Corinthians 12:28-30*

1. _____

2. _____
3. _____
4. _____
5. _____
6. _____
7. _____
8. _____

Two main categories of gifts are included in these passages. One group is made up of those which emphasize outward demonstrations which are clearly miraculous in nature. God gave them to the early church without preparation or development by the recipient. There are four such gifts listed above. List them below:

1. _____
2. _____
3. _____
4. _____

Gifts in the second category are supernatural because God gives the ability, energy, and productivity for them. However, they do not show themselves so clearly to be miraculous in nature. Thirteen such gifts are listed above, some of them in more than one passage. List the thirteen below:

1. _____
2. _____
3. _____
4. _____
5. _____
6. _____
7. _____
8. _____
9. _____
10. _____
11. _____
12. _____
13. _____

In addition to the above lists, several gifts are listed in Ephesians 4:11. They are sometimes called "office" gifts because they are thought of as positions in the church. They may be filled by persons showing any one of a number of spiritual gifts. For example, an evangelist may have the gift of preaching, exhortation, or possibly another speaking gift through which evangelism is accomplished. List the five "office" gifts below:

1. _____

2. _____

3. _____

4. _____

5. _____

Much of the writing about spiritual gifts has centered on the continuing debate regarding the four miraculous gifts and the five "office" gifts. The complex exegetical and theological issues involved in this debate can only be resolved by detailed studies. It is not the intent of this study to enter into these highly controversial areas. Our purpose is to assist the concerned Christian in determining which of the thirteen spiritual gifts he has. These gifts lend themselves to testing, evaluation, and service.

# TWO
# Understanding
# the Gifts

The first step toward discovering one's spiritual gift is to know what the gifts are. This may be accomplished in two ways. First, the biblical meaning of the words used to describe the gifts must be understood. This requires an analysis of the New Testament Greek words from which they are translated.

Second, the practical New Testament meaning of the words must be grasped. This is done by examining several passages in which the words are used. Insights from these passages will show what can be expected from the exercise of each gift.

Following is an examination of word meanings, together with illustrations from Scripture. Study the words, then answer the questions under "New Testament Insights."

## GIFT OF PROPHECY (PREACHING)
*Word meaning*

The biblical word "prophecy" (Romans 12:6) is translated from the Greek compound word, *prophateia,* which is made up of two parts: *pro,* "forth, for"; and *phateia,* "to speak." These parts combine to mean "to speak forth," or, in the noun form, "something spoken forth or one speaking forth." In the Old Testament, the prophets were God's mouthpiece for speaking forth his truth and his will to the people.

In the New Testament, there were prophets who spoke revelation to the infant church for the purpose of providing a foundation for the church (Ephesians 2:19-21). Later, others with the gift of prophecy spoke forth the Scripture with great conviction. The person with this gift strongly proclaimed the Scriptures with a view to seeing lives changed (1 Corinthians 14:3).

The gift of prophecy is evident in certain preachers today. The basic feature of speaking forth God's truth with strong feeling is still primary. However, since prophesying is a gift and not a position, professional preachers are not the only ones with the gift.

*New Testament insights*
1. What did the New Testament prophets do that indicated their gift?
   a. Luke 7:39_____
   b. Acts 11:28_____
   c. 1 Corinthians 14:24, 25_____
2. What specific inner motivations and goals did those with the gift of prophecy have?
   a. Acts 15:32_____
   b. 1 Corinthians 14:3_____
3. From Acts 13:1-5, what was Barnabas' and Saul's position and task (verse 1)?_____
   a. What did they do when they ministered (verse 5)?____

   b. Prophecy means "to speak forth" and preaching means "to herald the message." What do the two terms have in common?_____

4. As the New Testament was being completed, what provided the foundation for the prophet's proclamation? (See 2 Peter 1:19-21.)_____
5. How are true and false prophets distinguished?
   a. Deuteronomy 18:20-22_____
   b. Matthew 7:15, 16_____
   c. Matthew 24:23, 24_____

## GIFT OF TEACHING

*Word meaning*

The biblical word "teaching" (Romans 12:7) is translated from the Greek word *didasko,* meaning "to teach." The word has a very broad spectrum of meanings. It involves learning and understanding an area of knowledge. Also, it involves helping others to get from where they are in their understanding to where the teacher is.

The gifted teacher is one with great energy. He is concerned with designing and using the most effective methods for helping others to grasp truth. He is concerned with making the truth valuable for daily living.

*New Testament insights*
1. What was the central emphasis in all early church teaching? (See Acts 15:35; 18:11.)_____
2. What is the person with the gift of teaching concerned about?_____

19

    *a.* Acts 18:26_____

    *b.* Colossians 1:28; 3:16, 17_____

_____

3. How would you distinguish preaching from teaching? Both are mentioned together in various passages.
    *a.* Acts 5:42_____
    *b.* Acts 15:35_____
4. What concern bears on the heart of the truly gifted teacher? (See James 3:1.)_____

_____

## GIFT OF WORD OF KNOWLEDGE
*Word meaning*

The biblical word "knowledge" (1 Corinthians 12:8) is translated from the Greek word *ginosis.* It is the noun form of the often-used verb *ginosko,* "to know by observation [sight] and experience." It is to be distinguished from the other word for knowing, *oida,* "to know by the gathering and use of information" (having "heard").

One having the spiritual gift of the word of knowledge has a motivation for knowing the content of Scripture in detail. He understands and arranges truth carefully. The Holy Spirit enables him to have the proper balance and emphasis in viewing Scripture as a whole.

*New Testament insights*

From the following verses, indicate the areas of study which the one with the gift of the word of knowledge will develop:
    1. Luke 1:76-79_____
    2. Philippians 3:8_____
    3. 1 Corinthians 2:9-13_____
    4. 2 Corinthians 10:5_____

## GIFT OF WORD OF WISDOM
*Word meaning*

The biblical word "wisdom" (1 Corinthians 12:8) is translated from the Greek word *sophia,* meaning "wisdom," which derives from a root word meaning "to taste." This ties wisdom to experiential living rather than just to theory. Wisdom is the special ability to take a number of truths and use them to judge "gray areas" not directly resolved by a single truth.

One with the spiritual gift of wisdom and training demonstrates an unusual ability in the church to make discerning applications to practical questions on Christian living.

*New Testament insights*

1. The gift of wisdom will be based on what foundation?
   *a.* 1 Corinthians 1:23, 24, 30_____

   _____

   *b.* Ephesians 1:17_____

2. Characterize godly wisdom as shown in James 3:17. Then expand the meaning of each term to show how it helps a person be wise.

   *a.* _____
   *b.* _____
   *c.* _____
   *d.* _____
   *e.* _____
   *f.* _____
   *g.* _____
   *h.* _____

3. Using the Scripture verses below, indicate what words of wisdom can do for a church.

   *a.* Romans 16:19_____
   *b.* Ephesians 5:15, 17_____
   *c.* 2 Timothy 3:15_____

   _____

## GIFT OF EXHORTATION

*Word meaning*

The biblical word "exhortation" (Romans 12:8) is translated from the compound Greek word *paraklasis,* which is made up of the following two parts: *para,* "beside, alongside"; and *klasis,* "to call." The parts combine to mean "to call alongside"; or, in the noun form, "one called alongside another." In the broadest sense, one can be called alongside another for any number of reasons. The Bible narrows down the reasons for coming alongside to: (a) helping in a project, (b) embracing proper faith action, and (c) comforting others.

One with the spiritual gift of exhortation has the inner motivation and desire to encourage and comfort others in the above ways.

*A Practical Guide to Finding Your Spiritual Gifts*

*New Testament insights*

1. What is the main resource for their exhortations? (See Romans 15:4.)_____

2. What is the burden of the exhorter's heart?
   a. Acts 2:40_____
   b. Acts 11:23_____

3. What are some of the areas of life the New Testament exhorters spoke of in the exercise of exhortation?
   a. 1 Thessalonians 2:11, 12_____
   b. 1 Thessalonians 5:14_____
      _____
   c. Titus 1:9_____
   d. Hebrews 3:13_____

4. Barnabas was a classic example of a comforting, building exhorter. Note his special ministry to one man and the result. (See Acts 15:37-40; 2 Timothy 4:11.)_____
   _____
   _____

GIFT OF FAITH

*Word meaning*

The biblical word "faith" (1 Corinthians 12:9) is translated from one of the most common and basic New Testament words, *pistis,* which means "a trust or conviction about something or someone." As a spiritual gift, faith is confidence in God's wonder-working power. In 1 Corinthians 13:2 Paul writes: ". . . and though I have all faith *[pistis]* so that I could remove mountains . . ."

One with the spiritual gift of faith has vision and foresight. He demonstrates unusual confidence and boldness (Hebrews 11:1). Those with this gift serve to propel the body of believers into actively claiming the promises of God. Even when the church faces seemingly insurmountable problems, he is optimistic.

*New Testament insights*

1. Note some of the things accomplished by Old Testament saints who exercised great faith. (See Hebrews 11:33, 34.)_____
   _____
   _____

2. Read Acts 6:5-8. List the ways the gospel flourished through these men who were "full of faith."_____
   _____

3. Read Acts 11:22-24. Barnabas' faith produced what result in Christians and non-Christians?_____

_____

## GIFT OF DISCERNMENT OF SPIRITS
*Word meaning*

The biblical phrase "discerning of spirits" (1 Corinthians 12:10) is translated from the Greek words *diakrisis . . . pneumaton. Diakrisis* is a compound word made up of two parts: *dia,* "through"; and *krisis,* "to judge, divide, distinguish." The parts combine to mean one who "judges or distinguishes through a situation to a decision." *Pneumaton* is the normal word for spirits. When combined with *diakrisis,* it speaks of the process of judging through a person's speech and actions to discern the spirit behind them.

A person with the spiritual gift of discernment of spirits demonstrates a unique ability to correctly judge the true spiritual level and integrity of others.

*New Testament insights*
1. What two criteria are important for developing the gift of discernment of spirits? (See Hebrews 5:13, 14.)_____

_____

_____

2. What will be the inner drive of the one with this gift? (See 1 Thessalonians 5:21.)_____

_____

3. From the following passages, write down the situation briefly and the evidence of discernment of spirits.
   *a.* Acts 5:1-5_____

   _____

   *b.* Acts 8:18–23_____

   _____

   *c.* Acts 13:8-11_____

   _____

   *d.* Acts 16:16-18_____

   _____

   _____

4. Why is the gift of discernment of spirits so necessary in our day?
   *a.* 1 John 4:1-3_____
   *b.* 1 Timothy 4:1_____

   _____

## GIFT OF HELPS
*Word meaning*

The biblical word "helps" (1 Corinthians 12:28) is translated from the compound Greek word *antilapsis.* The word is made up of two parts: *anti,* "opposite, instead of and in exchange for"; and *lambano,* "to grasp, seize, or take up helpfully." The parts combine to mean in the noun form, "to seize something in front of one for the purpose of helping." This implies responding to a request to do a certain job. Such usage was prevalent in early papyrus writings.

One with the spiritual gift of helps responds when a need becomes clearly known and a request for help is given.

*New Testament insights*

From the Scriptures below, describe some of the people with this gift and what they did.
   1. Acts 20:35_____
   2. 1 Timothy 6:2_____
   3. 2 Timothy 1:16_____
   4. 1 Corinthians 16:15_____

   _____

## GIFT OF SERVING (MINISTRY)
*Word meaning*

The biblical word for "serving" or "ministry" (Romans 12:7) is translated from the Greek word *diakonos.* The word "deacon" in the New Testament comes directly from it. It is probably derived from the verb *dioko,* "to hasten after, pursue."

There are many Greek words translated "service." One emphasizes the subjection of the server to his master; another, the willingness to serve due to high respect; and another, service for wages. In contrast, *diakonos* conveys the idea of very special and personal service rendered to another in love.

One with the spiritual gift of serving is motivated to

initiate service for another in the body of Christ. He will serve diligently in love.

*New Testament insights*
From the Scripture verses below, describe some of the qualities, activities, and results of one having the gift of serving:
1. Luke 10:40_____
2. Luke 22:27_____
3. Acts 6:1-3_____
4. Romans 16:1, 2_____
5. 1 Corinthians 16:15-18_____
6. Colossians 4:7, 8_____

## GIFT OF ADMINISTRATION (GOVERNMENTS)
*Word meaning*
The biblical word "governments" (1 Corinthians 12:28) is translated from the Greek word *kubernesis,* meaning "to guide, govern." It was specifically used of a helmsman of a ship. His position was the most important in determining the direction of the ship (James 3:4).

One with the spiritual gift of administration or government manifests the wisdom, tact, and decisiveness to give guidance to one or many aspects of the church work.

*New Testament insights*
The only New Testament uses of the word other than that in 1 Corinthians 12:28 are Acts 27:11 and Revelation 18:17, both of which refer to the "master" of a ship. Using the account in Acts 27:11-20; 27-29; 38-44, write down the decisions made by the master helmsman during the storm.

1. _____
2. _____
3. _____
4. _____
5. _____
6. _____
7. _____
8. _____
9. _____
10. _____
11. _____

12. _____

13. _____

14. _____

Obviously the helmsman in the above situation was operating under great stress. Had he obeyed Paul's early warning not to start out on the journey, he would not have had the problems. However, from the list of decisions the helmsman made, draw out some principles that a gifted administrator in a church should use. Some of the principles may be derived from what the helmsman did wrong.

1. _____

2. _____

3. _____

4. _____

5. _____

6. _____

7. _____

8. _____

## GIFT OF RULING

*Word meaning*

The biblical word "ruling" (Romans 12:8) is translated from the compound Greek word *prohistame,* made up of the following two parts: *pro,* "before"; and *histame,* "to stand." The parts combine to mean "to stand before" others for the purpose of overseeing or directing work.

One with the spiritual gift of ruling manifests the confidence, desire, and skills required to lead a group.

*New Testament insights*

1. How should the ruler rule? (See 1 Timothy 3:4, 5, 12.)___

_____

2. What characterizes the ruler's leadership? (See 1 Thessalonians 5:12, 13.)_____

3. What is one of the ongoing tasks of the ruler? (See Titus 1:5.)_____

4. What is the foundation for proper ruling? (See 1 Timothy 5:17.)_____

## GIFT OF MERCY

*Word meaning*

The biblical word "mercy" (Romans 12:8) is translated

from the Greek word *eleon*, meaning "mercy, pathos."
Webster's dictionary defines pathos as "the quality in
something experienced or observed which arouses feelings
of pity, sorrow, sympathy, or compassion." These feelings
provide the motivation for action in one with this gift.

One with the spiritual gift of mercy cheerfully
demonstrates in action compassion for those that are sick
or in misery, either physically or spiritually.

*New Testament insights*
1. What actions constituted acts of mercy in the following
   passages?
   *a.* From Luke 10:30-37, indicate the progression of four
   specific actions taken by this merciful man.
   *1)* _____
   *2)* _____
   *3)* _____
   *4)* _____
   *b.* Philippians 2:1-3_____
2. What attitude should characterize acts of mercy? (See
   Romans 12:8.)_____
3. What should be the outstanding motivation for acting in
   mercy toward others? (See Titus 3:5.)_____
   _____

## GIFT OF GIVING
*Word meaning*
   The biblical word "giving" (Romans 12:8) is translated
from the compound Greek word *metadidomi*. It is made up
of two parts: *meta,* "in the midst of, in association or
fellowship"; and *didomi,* "to give." The parts combine to
mean "to give in association with others." It implies that
the giving is not done objectively or coldly, but within the
context of a spiritual relationship.

   There is fellowship with God in giving as an act of
worship. There is fellowship with others when giving is
done in love and concern for the needy.

   One with the spiritual gift of giving has the inner
motivation and desire to share in others' needs by giving
of himself, his material goods and money.

*New Testament insights*
1. What is the main viewpoint to have in exercising the
   gift of giving? (See 2 Corinthians 8:4.)_____
   _____

2. What is the main purpose for the gift of giving in the body of Christ? (See Ephesians 4:28.)_____

_____

3. What kind of needs are met by one with the gift of giving?
   a. Matthew 6:1-4_____
   b. Luke 3:11_____
   c. Acts 11:27-30_____
4. What are some of the attitudes toward giving that we might expect to see in someone with the gift?
   a. 2 Corinthians 8:12_____
   b. 2 Corinthians 9:7_____
   c. 2 Corinthians 9:13_____

HOW MANY GIFTS DO I HAVE? A central question which has not yet been totally resolved by biblical scholars is: Is it possible for a believer to have more than one unique spiritual gift? A brief survey of the Scriptures involved will suffice to show that every believer has at least one spiritual gift.

In 1 Peter 4:10 (NASB), Peter writes, ". . . as each one has received a special gift . . ." In addition, the body metaphor, as developed by Paul in 1 Corinthians 12:12-27, Romans 12:4, 5 and Ephesians 4:12-16, emphasizes that the gifted members of the church are similar to the functioning parts of the physical body. Each physical member of the body has a unique function to fulfill for the proper working of the body. Likewise, it is argued, each spiritual member of the spiritual body, the church, has a unique function (as a spiritually gifted believer) to fulfill for the proper working of the whole spiritual body.

In addition, those who believe that every Christian has just one gift point out that the word "severally" in 1 Corinthians 12:11 (". . . the selfsame Spirit, dividing to every man severally as he will," KJV), should be translated "individually." This removes the implication from the verse that the Spirit may give several gifts to one believer.

Others believe that a Christian may have more than one spiritual gift. They appeal to the fact that Paul, for example, had a number of spiritual gifts, such as prophecy, teaching, miracles, tongues, etc. They argue that in using the body metaphor, Paul was simply trying to show the interrelationship and necessity of the various spiritual gifts in the church. They contend he was not trying to speak to the issue of the number of gifts one member in that body might have.

Finally, those who believe that a Christian may have more than one gift take 1 Corinthians 12:31 ("But covet earnestly the best gifts") as an imperative command to seek the best gifts. If it is possible to seek gifts (plural) and receive them, it must also be possible to have more than one gift by such seeking.

The above discussion will suffice to show the nature of the debate on the issue. For purposes of this study, reference will be made to "gift" rather than to "gifts" since we are confident that each believer has at least one spiritual gift.

# THREE
## The Trinity at Work in the Gifted Church

All three Persons of the eternal Godhead—God the Father, God the Son, and God the Holy Spirit—are involved in spiritual gifts. This is a clear testimony to their unity in essence and purpose and yet their distinctiveness in personality and activity. While they have the same eternal attributes, each of the three Persons has unique ministries which distinguish him from the others. An understanding of the Trinity's working is an essential foundation for putting spiritual gifts in proper perspective.

In this chapter we shall study the members of the Trinity as they are revealed in the major passages on spiritual gifts. Other passages will be included only for expansion and clarification.

GOD THE FATHER

*1.* In Ephesians 4:6, the word "all" refers to the believers in the "one body" mentioned in 4:4. Therefore, God is the Father of all the individuals in the church body. From verse 6, list the four ways God is related to all the believers. Then, using the additional verses given, explain some of the details of his leadership.

  *a.* _____
      Ephesians 1:2, 3_____
      Ephesians 2:19_____
      _____
      Ephesians 3:14, 15_____
      _____
      2 Corinthians 6:17, 18_____
      _____

  *b.* _____
      Psalm 57:5_____
      James 1:17_____
      _____

  *c.* _____
      1 Corinthians 8:6_____
      _____
      1 Timothy 2:5_____
      _____

  *d.* _____

John 14:17_____

_____

1 Corinthians 6:19_____

_____

2. What attribute of God the Father makes him willing to exercise headship over men by a personal relationship with them? (See Romans 12:1a.)_____

_____

   a. Did God have to provide for this relationship?
     2 Peter 2:4-7_____

     _____

     Titus 3:3-7_____

     _____

   b. What is the key character quality the Father desires to develop in those with whom he has a relationship? (See Leviticus 11:44.)_____
3. The way in which God's mercy is displayed in the church is worked out in what is called his_____
(Romans 12:2).

## GOD THE SON
1. To fulfill God's will within the church, the believer must first commit himself to what position concerning Jesus Christ? (See 1 Corinthians 12:3.)_____
   a. What is involved in making and keeping this commitment?
     Luke 6:46_____
     John 11:27_____
     2 Corinthians 6:17_____
     Colossians 1:10_____
2. What two main goals should every Christian strive for in his relationship with Christ? (See Ephesians 4:13).

   a. _____
     Ephesians 4:3-6_____

     _____

     Ephesians 1:17_____

     _____

     Philippians 3:8-10_____

     _____

   b. _____
     John 1:14_____

     _____

3. What are the respective tasks of Christ and Christians within the church?

*A Practical Guide to Finding Your Spiritual Gifts*

    *a.* Ephesians 4:15, 16_____

_____

    *b.* Acts 2:47_____

_____

    *c.* Romans 12:5_____

_____

    *d.* 1 Corinthians 12:27_____

_____

## GOD THE HOLY SPIRIT

1. What is the Spirit's contribution toward the believer's entrance into the body of Christ?

    *a.* John 3:5_____

_____

    *b.* 1 Corinthians 12:13_____

_____

2. What is the Holy Spirit's main goal in working with gifted believers in the body of Christ? (See Ephesians 4:3.)_____

_____

_____

## SUMMARY

Summarize briefly the main tasks of the Father, Son, and Holy Spirit pertaining to the Christian in the church.

*God the Father:*

_____

_____

_____

_____

*God the Son:*

_____

_____

_____

_____

*God the Holy Spirit:*

_____

_____

_____

_____

# FOUR
## The Trinity at Work
## with the Gifts

The Trinity is at work not only in the growth and
development of the Church, but also in the introduction
and integration of the spiritual gifts into local churches.
Study the verses which indicate the Trinity's involvement
in establishing a church of gifted believers. Explain briefly
the meaning of each verse.

GOD THE FATHER
1. Romans 12:3_____

_____

2. 1 Corinthians 12:6_____

_____

3. 1 Corinthians 12:18_____

_____

4. 1 Corinthians 12:24_____

_____

GOD THE SON
1. 1 Corinthians 12:5_____

_____

GOD THE HOLY SPIRIT
1. 1 Corinthians 12:4, 11_____

_____

_____

SUMMARY
   Summarize in the most logical progression (starting with
first things first) the six contributions of the Trinity
toward establishing the gift of each believer in the church
body.
1. _____
2. _____
3. _____
4. _____
5. _____
6. _____

   At what points in this process can the believer thwart
what the Godhead wants to do with his gift in the church?
1. _____

2. _____

3. _____

4. _____

What do you think happens to a church when contributions by the Trinity cannot materialize due to a believer's inactivity?_____

_____

_____

# FIVE
## Studying
## the Key Passages

Four key passages in the New Testament give us the main biblical principles about thirteen spiritual gifts and their part in the church. These texts are Romans 12:1-8; 1 Corinthians 12:1-31; Ephesians 4:1-16; and 1 Peter 4:7-11. We shall study these passages under three topical headings. In addition, other individual verses where spiritual gifts *(charismata)* are referred to will be examined to gain as complete a biblical understanding as possible.

### PERSONAL PREPARATION BEFORE USING SPIRITUAL GIFTS

*1.* What four critical commitments must be made before a person should try to determine his spiritual gift? (See Romans 12:1-3.)

*a.* _____

*b.* _____

*c.* _____

*d.* _____

*2.* What Jewish practice was in Paul's thinking in Romans 12:1 when he wrote, "present your bodies"? (See Luke 2:22.)_____

*3.* How can we parallel today the presentation explained in Luke 2:22, since we no longer do that?_____

*4.* A "living sacrifice" (Romans 12:1) is a contradiction in terms unless one can die and still be alive. In what sense is the consecrated believer alive and dead? (See Romans 6:6-9, 11-13.)_____

*5.* What is "acceptable unto God" (Romans 12:1) in a New Testament life sacrifice? (See Acts 10:35.)_____

*6.* What does it mean to be "conformed" to this world? (Romans 12:2.)

*a.* Ephesians 2:2, 3_____

    *b.* John 2:16 _____

_____

7. A transformation is what takes place in a caterpillar
   when it goes through metamorphosis and becomes a
   butterfly. It is an inner transformation with an outer
   manifestation. How does the inner, spiritual
   transformation take place in the consecrated believer in
   Jesus Christ?
   *a.* Romans 12:2b _____
   *b.* Philippians 4:8 _____

   _____

8. While the transformation process is going on, we should
   be able to determine with confidence the will of God.
   How can we know the will of God? What specific things
   are the will of God?
   *a.* John 7:17 _____

   _____

   *b.* 1 Thessalonians 4:3 _____
   *c.* 1 Thessalonians 5:18 _____
   *d.* 1 Peter 2:15 _____

9. What characterizes a "worthy" walk for the believer in
   relationship to his local church? (See Ephesians 4:2.) To
   the right of your answer, give the positive results of
   such a walk in the church life; give also the negative
   results of doing the opposite.

   |  | *Positive* | *Negative* |
   |---|---|---|
   | *a.* _____ | _____ | _____ |
   | *b.* _____ | _____ | _____ |
   | *c.* _____ | _____ | _____ |
   | *d.* _____ | _____ | _____ |

10. Peter gives four essential qualities in 1 Peter 4:7-9 as
    preliminary considerations before discussing the use of
    one's spiritual gift. List them and explain briefly what
    each quality means, using a dictionary to define the
    terms.
    *a.* _____

    _____

    *b.* _____

c. _____
_____

d. _____
_____

11. Note briefly how each of the qualities in question 10 will help one in finding and/or using his spiritual gift.

   a. _____
   _____

   b. _____
   _____

   c. _____
   _____

   d. _____
   _____

## MORE BIBLICAL INSIGHTS ABOUT THE GIFTS

1. In 1 Peter 4:10 we find three very important principles regarding spiritual gifts. What are they?

   a. _____
   b. _____
   c. _____

2. What is a steward? (See 1 Peter 4:10.) Give a modern-day example.

   _____

   a. Does a steward own that with which he works? What implications does your answer hold for your understanding of a spiritual gift?_____

   _____

   b. What character qualities would you look for if you were going to hire a steward?_____

   _____

   c. What is a steward's main responsibility according to 1 Corinthians 4:2, and how does this responsibility apply to the believer's spiritual gift?_____

   _____

3. What is Peter expressing in 1 Peter 4:11 about the exercise of the believer's gift?_____

   _____

    *a.* How does one accomplish this goal: "that God may be glorified through Jesus Christ"?
Ephesians 5:18_____
1 Peter 2:12_____
1 John 1:9_____

    *b.* What tendency in man is Peter warning the believer about in verse 11?_____

          _____

*4.* What does Romans 11:29 add to our understanding about God and his relationship to spiritual gifts?_____

          _____

*5.* There are other "grace gifts" from God mentioned in the New Testament which are not in the same category as the special spiritual gifts given to the church. Note them from the Scriptures below.
    *a.* Romans 5:15, 16; 6:23_____
    *b.* 1 Corinthians 7:7_____
    *c.* 2 Corinthians 1:8-11_____

          _____

*6.* What stern warning does Paul give to Timothy in 1 Timothy 4:14 regarding his gift? _____

    Why is it important to heed this warning? (See Luke 12:35-48.)_____

          _____

*7.* Read 2 Timothy 1:3-11. What encouragement does Paul give Timothy in verse 6 that we should remember too?__

          _____

          _____

## THE GIFTS WORKING TOGETHER IN THE CHURCH

*1.* In 1 Corinthians 7:7 it says that the whole church profits when each believer is properly using his gift. How does the church profit?_____

          _____

*2.* Give a summary statement of what Paul is expressing in 1 Corinthians 12:20-25 with regard to gifts in the church.

          _____

          _____

          _____

*3.* What does 1 Corinthians 12:26 tell us should be happening when gifted church members are all ministering?_____

_____

4. What are the two key goals for every church body as
   given in Ephesians 4:3? Explain what each phrase
   means in practical terms.

   *a.* _____

   _____

   *b.* _____

   _____

5. What is the crucial task given to the evangelists,
   pastors, and teachers according to Ephesians 4:12?_____

   _____

   *a.* In light of the above directive, do you think
   evangelists should be holding mass meetings around
   the world, or should they be involved in the local
   churches, training and teaching others to share their
   faith?_____

   _____

   *b.* Also, in light of the task given to pastors and
   teachers, should the church be hiring pastors and
   teachers to do the major share of the ministering?
   Why or why not?_____

   _____

   *c.* After the perfecting and ministry are progressing,
   what purpose do the gifts serve in the church? (See
   Ephesians 4:12c.)_____

   _____

6. What end goals are desired for every church member
   when the gifted believers are ministering to one
   another? (See Ephesians 4:13-17.)

   *a.* _____
   *b.* _____
   *c.* _____
   *d.* _____
   *e.* _____
   *f.* _____

7. Can the goals of verse 13 ever be realized in this life, or
   is Paul setting forth a utopian ideal never attainable
   this side of heaven? Explain your answer, using
   Ephesians 3:19; Colossians 1:9-11; 2:6, 7; Philippians
   1:9-11.

_____

_____

_____

8. What emphasis will need to be supplied in the gifted church to insure that there will be no "tossed children" as noted in Ephesians 4:14; Hebrews 5:12—6:2?_____

_____

_____

9. What principle regarding the gifts in their relationship to the local church can we derive from 1 Corinthians 1:7?

_____

_____

_____

# SIX
# Evaluation One:
# Your Spiritual Interests

How can you recognize your spiritual gift? As a Christian, your thoughts, preferences, attitudes, emotional reactions, and past and present service experiences will probably indicate your spiritual gift. By analyzing the exact makeup of these indicators, you can obtain insight that will help you determine your gift.

The greatest difficulty in forming an evaluation method is in trying to construct a procedure that will indicate your spiritual preferences and motivations rather than merely your natural talents and abilities. Because of the complexity of this challenge, no single evaluation or group of evaluations will indicate your gift. You can confirm any tentative conclusions only by actually serving. Therefore, the following evaluations are simply to help you narrow down the number of gifts you will need to test through serving.

## PERSONAL ASSESSMENT
## OF PREFERENCES AND TENDENCIES
*Instructions:*
A. Circle as many answers to each question as solidly apply to you. DO NOT LIMIT YOUR RESPONSE TO ONE CHOICE if more than one applies, unless a specific limitation is given along with the question.
B. Circle no response if you find that none of the choices apply to you. For example, if you prefer not to speak or make presentations, do not circle any of the answers in question 4.
  1. I prefer situations in my church in which I am:
     *a.* a speaker
     *b.* in a discussion group
     *c.* just a listener
  2. If asked to speak, I prefer to speak to:
     *a.* large groups
     *b.* small groups
     *c.* individuals
  3. When faced with counseling another person about his or her problems, I tend to:
     *a.* identify deeply with that person's situation

  *b.* offer the best biblical solution I can think of, even if I'm not totally confident about my counsel

  *c.* prefer sharing biblical insights, while avoiding discussions about feelings

  *d.* urge him/her to follow my counsel, because I honestly believe God often helps me see solutions to others' problems

4. When I begin to prepare to speak to other Christians, I am normally motivated to:

  *a.* emphasize the truths of basic Bible themes so as to lead the listeners to a clear-cut decision in the meeting

  *b.* carefully organize a biblical passage in a systematic way so that the listeners can clearly understand its meaning

  *c.* instruct on doctrinal topics to enable the listeners to have a better understanding of these subject areas

  *d.* stress application of passages that emphasize practical truths, so that the listener's conduct can be refined

  *e.* take one verse, and outline practical, specific steps of action for the listeners to follow

5. When listening to others speak, I tend to:

  *a.* dislike in-depth doctrinal studies without applications

  *b.* dislike talks which heavily emphasize illustrations and applications, without logical order and doctrine.

  *c.* be strongly impressed by exhortations to serve other Christians

6. If I had to choose between the following approaches to personal devotions, I most prefer to (choose only one response):

  *a.* search out how the verses I'm studying add to my understanding of doctrine

  *b.* analyze the verses with the purpose of changing specific areas of my conduct

  *c.* relate to the verses emotionally, so as to get a personal blessing

7. If I had my choice of passages to study, I would

usually choose ones which (choose only one response):
   a. are rich in doctrine
   b. are very practical
   c. are controversial or difficult to understand
   d. have great emotional appeal to my Christian life

8. When I give a testimony, I tend to:
   a. encourage or console others, rather than just share a verse or experience
   b. indicate some area of doctrine that has come alive to me through an experience and/or verse I've studied
   c. emphasize the practical applications of some verses to my life

9. With regard to planning for the future of my church, I tend to:
   a. have positive confidence about what the church should do
   b. be concerned about and willing to do detailed, deliberate work on the plans
   c. be more concerned with envisioning end results than with the details involved in getting there
   d. have a great desire to see quick growth in the ministries of the church

10. When conversing with other Christians, I tend to:
   a. probe them to determine their true spiritual condition and needs
   b. exhort them to embrace certain goals and actions

11. If a person were to ask me to evaluate his or her spiritual condition, I would tend to:
   a. point out errors in his or her mental understanding of the Christian life and doctrine
   b. sense areas of right and wrong conduct in that person's life, and point out some solutions
   c. be critical of areas of the person's life which are not disciplined and well ordered

12. When presented with a physical or spiritual need, I tend to:
   a. respond on my own initiative to try to meet it if possible

    *b.* respond best if someone calls and asks me to help fill it

    *c.* not respond if the need requires considerable personal preparation

    *d.* not respond if the need involves a lot of organizational detail and red tape

    *e.* respond with money and possessions

*13.* In an organization, I usually prefer to (choose only one response):

    *a.* lead a group

    *b.* be a follower under another's leadership

*14.* When given a task which needs to be done now, I:

    *a.* tend to complete it before taking on another task

    *b.* tend to leave it for another task if the second one seems more important at the time

    *c.* prefer to be told by a competent leader exactly what to do

    *d.* tend to be concerned with doing a high quality and thorough job

    *e.* favor doing it myself rather than delegating it

*15.* If asked to lead in a church program somewhere, I would tend to choose a position which involves:

    *a.* comprehensive planning for the future

    *b.* detailed planning and decision making for the present

    *c.* harmonizing various viewpoints for a decision

    *d.* evaluating personnel for various leadership positions

    *e.* drawing up procedures and guidelines for effective inner working of the church

    *f.* delegating responsibilities to others

*16.* If a group is meeting and no assigned leader is there, I would tend to:

    *a.* assume the leadership

    *b.* let the meeting proceed with no direct leadership

    *c.* appoint or ask someone in the group to lead

    *d.* call someone to find out who the real leader is

*17.* My reaction to the needs of others tends to be:

    *a.* slow, because I don't know what to do

    *b.* quick, because I sense what needs to be done most of the time

c. deliberate, because I want to make sure I've thought it through thoroughly

18. In regard to decision making when the facts are clear, I tend to:
    a. make decisions easily and with confidence
    b. lack firmness because of people's feelings
    c. rely on others whom I believe are more capable of sorting out the issues in the decision

19. With regard to financial matters, I tend to:
    a. be able to make wise investments and gain wealth
    b. be moved to give all I can to people and organizations I consider worthy
    c. want assurances that the money I give will be used wisely
    d. feel deeply that such matters should be handled in an orderly and prudent manner
    e. see money as a means for carrying out ministries and meeting needs, more than for construction of buildings, payment of salaries, etc.
    f. work hard to meet legitimate needs

20. If given a choice among the following involvements in a Sunday school class lesson, I would most favor (choose only one response):
    a. doing the biblical research and study to provide the lesson content
    b. organizing available content and illustrations for presentation of the truths
    c. thinking up original applications for the lesson after having been given the organized content
    d. presenting the lesson for which the content, illustrations, and applications are provided

21. With regard to decisions made from my speaking, I prefer to (choose only one response):
    a. see an immediate commitment at the meeting by individuals in the group
    b. do follow-up counseling directed at long-run changes in conduct
    c. have an opportunity to explore the decision in depth through discussion

22. If I were a leader faced with two Christians in the

church who couldn't get along, I would tend to
(choose only one response):
- *a.* change one person's responsibilities and
  position at the point of conflict
- *b.* talk to the two people about changing their
  attitudes
- *c.* leave the situation alone, for fear of offending
  and making it worse

23. When called upon to serve, I am most naturally
motivated to help in situations in which there are
specific:
- *a.* material needs (food, buildings, equipment,
  money)
- *b.* mental needs (lack of understanding of
  Scripture, need to find God's will in a certain
  matter, etc.)
- *c.* emotional needs (fear, anxiety, frustration,
  moods due to pain and trials, etc.)
- *d.* spiritual needs (for commitment, faith, dealing
  with sin, etc.)

24. When speaking before people, I:
- *a.* sense an inner urgency to persuade people to
  make spiritual decisions and commitments
  right then
- *b.* find it easy to accept the authority of the
  Scriptures without hesitation
- *c.* am inwardly compelled to prepare well and
  speak carefully
- *d.* encourage thought-life decisions more than
  conduct changes
- *e.* feel most comfortable presenting a thorough,
  detailed study of a biblical passage or topic
- *f.* have an inner urge to share practical insights
  consistent with high biblical standards
- *g.* have a tendency to feel real concern for those
  in difficulty, and to suggest ways to help them

25. Generally speaking, I have a tendency to:
- *a.* visualize future goals and work toward them in
  spite of the difficulties
- *b.* be wise in discerning the character quality of
  another person
- *c.* accurately detect weaknesses and pitfalls when
  evaluating opportunities and situations

    *d.* have great energy and stamina for working on
and meeting the practical needs of others

    *e.* be sensitive to overall organizational direction
more than minority, individual opinions

    *f.* help meet obvious needs without measuring the
worthiness of the recipient or evaluating his
real needs

    *g.* desire positive results and high quality in the
things to which I give my efforts and money

    *h.* see through others' actions to their real motives
and inner attitudes

## SCORE SHEET FOR PERSONAL ASSESSMENT OF PREFERENCES AND TENDENCIES

*Instructions:*

1. In the far left-hand column of this score sheet is a list
of all the possible responses for the multiple choice
questionnaire (1a, 1b, 1c, etc.). Transfer the circled
answers from your questionnaire to this score sheet
by circling the number-letter of each answer in the
left-hand column that you circled in the
questionnaire.

2. Each circled answer indicates an element of
preference for one or more spiritual gifts. The
spiritual gifts preferred by a given answer are
indicated by an X in the boxes to the right of the
response. For example, if you circled the answer 1a in
the questionnaire, it indicates that you prefer
preaching, teaching, and ruling, since the X's in the
boxes to the right of 1a fall in the columns for those
gifts.

3. Circle every X that you see as you move from the
circled answers at the left across the page to your
right. Do this for each circled response in the
left-hand column.

4. Now, go to the end of the score sheet and notice that
you must enter the total number of circled X's for
each gift. To do this, count the circled X's in each gift
column and enter the total in the box provided.

5. Then, go to the percentage equivalent chart at the
end of the score sheet. Find the percentage equivalent
to the number circled and enter it in the "% CIRCLED"
box below the "TOTAL CIRCLED" box.

6. The top three or four percentages will indicate the gifts toward which you seem to show the greatest preference and tendency. List those gifts in order, starting with the one(s) with the highest percentage, on page 77, under 1.
7. See Appendix III if you have difficulty scoring the questionnaire.

| | PREACHING | TEACHING | KNOWLEDGE | WISDOM | EXHORTATION | FAITH | DISCERNMENT OF SPIRITS | HELPS | SERVING | ADMINISTRATION | RULING | MERCY | GIVING |
|---|---|---|---|---|---|---|---|---|---|---|---|---|---|
| 1a | X | X | | | | | | | | | X | | |
| 1b | | X | X | X | X | X | X | | | X | | | |
| 1c | | | | | | | | | | | | X | |
| 2a | X | X | | | X | | | | | | | | |
| 2b | | X | X | X | | X | X | | | X | | | |
| 2c | | | | X | | | | X | | | | X | |
| 3a | | | | X | | | | X | X | | | X | X |
| 3b | X | X | | | | X | | | | | X | X | |
| 3c | | | X | | | | | | | | | | |
| 3d | | | | | X | X | | X | | | | | |
| 4a | X | | | | | | | | | | | | |
| 4b | | X | | | | | | | | | | | |
| 4c | | | X | | | | | | | | | | |
| 4d | | | | X | | | | | | | | | |
| 4e | | | | | X | | | | | | | | |
| 5a | | | | | X | X | | X | X | | | | X |
| 5b | | X | X | | | | | | | | X | X | |
| 5c | | | | | | | | X | X | | | | X |
| 6a | | X | X | | | | | | | | | | |
| 6b | | | | | X | X | | X | | | | | |
| 6c | X | | | | | X | | X | X | | | X | X |
| 7a | | X | X | | | | | | | | | | |
| 7b | X | | | | X | X | X | | X | X | | X | X |
| 7c | | X | X | | | | X | | | | | | |
| 7d | X | | | | | | | | | | | X | |
| 8a | | | | | X | X | | | | | | X | |
| 8b | X | X | X | | | | | | | | | | |
| 8c | X | | | | X | | | X | X | X | | | |

| PREACHING | TEACHING | KNOWLEDGE | WISDOM | EXHORTATION | FAITH | DISCERNMENT OF SPIRITS | HELPS | SERVING | ADMINISTRATION | RULING | MERCY | GIVING | |
|---|---|---|---|---|---|---|---|---|---|---|---|---|---|
| | | | | | X | | | | | | | | 9a |
| | | | | | | | | | X | | | | 9b |
| | | | | X | | | | | | | | | 9c |
| | | | | X | | | | | | | | | 9d |
| | | | | | | X | | | | | | | 10a |
| | | | | X | X | | | | | | | | 10b |
| | | | | | | | | | | | | | 10c |
| X | X | X | | | | | | | | | | | 11a |
| | | | | X | | X | | | | | | | 11b |
| | | | | | | | | | X | X | | | 11c |
| | | | | | | | | X | | | | X | 12a |
| | | | | | | | X | | | | | | 12b |
| | | | | | | | X | | | | | | 12c |
| | | | | | | | X | X | | | | | 12d |
| | | | | | | | | | | | | X | 12e |
| X | | | | | | | | X | X | X | | | 13a |
| | | | | | | | X | | | | X | | 13b |
| | | | | | | | | | X | X | | | 14a |
| | | | | | | | | X | | | | | 14b |
| | | | | | | | X | | | | | | 14c |
| | | | | | | | | X | X | X | | | 14d |
| | | | | | | | X | X | | | X | X | 14e |
| | | | | | X | | | | | | | | 15a |
| | | | | | | | | | X | | | | 15b |
| | | | | | | | | | X | X | | | 15c |
| | | | | | | X | | | | | | | 15d |
| | | | | | | | | | X | | | | 15e |
| | | | | | | | | | | X | | | 15f |
| | | | | | | | | X | | X | | | 16a |
| | | | | | | | X | | | | | | 16b |
| | | | | | | | | | X | | | | 16c |
| | | | X | | | | | | | | | | 16d |
| | | X | | | | | | | | | | | 17a |
| | | | | X | X | | | X | | | X | X | 17b |
| | | | X | | | X | | | X | X | | | 17c |
| | | | | | | X | | | X | X | | | 18a |
| | | | | | | | | | | | X | | 18b |

49

| | PREACHING | TEACHING | KNOWLEDGE | WISDOM | EXHORTATION | FAITH | DISCERNMENT OF SPIRITS | HELPS | SERVING | ADMINISTRATION | RULING | MERCY | GIVING |
|---|---|---|---|---|---|---|---|---|---|---|---|---|---|
| 18c | | | | | | | | X | | | | | |
| 19a | | | | | | | | | | | | | X |
| 19b | | | | | | | | | | | | | X |
| 19c | | | | | | | | | | | | | X |
| 19d | | | | | | | | | | X | X | | X |
| 19e | | | | | X | | | | | | | | |
| 19f | | | | | | | | | | | | | X |
| 20a | | | X | | | | | | | | | | |
| 20b | | X | | | | | | | | | | | |
| 20c | | | | X | | | | | | | | | |
| 20d | X | | | | | | | | | | | | |
| 21a | X | | | | | X | | | | | | | |
| 21b | | | | X | X | | | | | | | | |
| 21c | | X | X | | | | X | | | | | | |
| 22a | | | | | | | | | | X | X | | |
| 22b | | | | X | X | | | | | | | | |
| 22c | | | | | | | | | | | | X | |
| 23a | | | | | | | | X | X | X | X | | X |
| 23b | | X | X | X | | | | | | | | | |
| 23c | | | | | X | | | | | | X | | |
| 23d | X | | | | | X | X | | | | | | |
| 24a | X | | | | | | | | | | | | |
| 24b | X | | | | | | | | | | | | |
| 24c | | X | | | | | | | | | | | |
| 24d | | | X | | | | | | | | | | |
| 24e | | | X | | | | | | | | | | |
| 24f | | | | X | | | | | | | | | |
| 24g | | | | | X | | | | | | | | |
| 25a | | | | | | X | | | | | | | |
| 25b | | | | | | | X | | | | | | |
| 25c | | | | | | | X | | | | | | |
| 25d | | | | | | | | | | X | | | |
| 25e | | | | | | | | | | | X | | |
| 25f | | | | | | | | | | | | X | |
| 25g | | | | | | | | | | | | | X |
| 25h | | | | | | | X | | | | | | |

TOTAL
CIRCLED

_____

%
CIRCLED

_____

| | Total Circled | % | Total Circled | % |
|---|---|---|---|---|
| PERCENTAGES | 1 | 6 | 9 | 56 |
| | 2 | 13 | 10 | 63 |
| | 3 | 19 | 11 | 69 |
| | 4 | 25 | 12 | 75 |
| | 5 | 31 | 13 | 81 |
| | 6 | 38 | 14 | 88 |
| | 7 | 44 | 15 | 94 |
| | 8 | 50 | 16 | 100 |

**NOTE: If your results are the same or similar for three or four gifts, go to Appendix IV for evaluation of the results.**

# SEVEN
## Evaluation Two:
## Spiritual Interests
## Others See in You

No person is totally objective about himself. His self-image affects his viewpoint about his natural talents. The same is true about his spiritual gifts. Therefore, it is helpful to have others participate in the determination of what our spiritual gifts are.

The following questionnaire should be filled in by the four Christians who know you best. One's parents and one's marriage partner should definitely be considered for this purpose. Then, choose others on the basis of the length of time they have known you, and the depth of your friendship with them.

After you have received the completed questionnaires and scored them, analyze the results to see whether any gifts appear to be predominant. Enter those gifts on page 78.

If the score sheet indicates that three or four gifts have the same or very similar percentages, go to Appendix V for help in evaluating the results.

OTHERS' ASSESSMENT
OF PREFERENCES AND TENDENCIES
*Instructions:*
- A. Circle as many answers to each question as solidly apply to the person you are evaluating. DO NOT LIMIT YOUR RESPONSE TO ONE CHOICE if more than one applies, unless a specific limitation is given along with the question.
- B. Circle no response if you find that none of the choices apply. For example, if you believe that the person prefers not to speak or make presentations, do not circle any of the answers in question 4.
  - *1.* He/she prefers situations in the church in which he/she is:
    - *a.* a speaker
    - *b.* in a discussion group
    - *c.* just a listener
  - *2.* If asked to speak, he/she prefers to speak to:

a. large groups
b. small groups
c. individuals

3. When faced with counseling another person about problems, he/she tends to:
   a. identify deeply with the other person's situation
   b. give the other person the best biblical solution he/she can think of, even if not totally confident about the counsel
   c. prefer sharing biblical insights, avoiding discussions about feelings
   d. urge the person to follow his/her counsel, because he/she honestly believes God helps him/her see the solutions to others' problems

4. When preparing for talks to other Christians, he/she is normally motivated to:
   a. emphasize the truths of basic Bible themes, so as to lead the listeners to a clear-cut decision in the meeting
   b. carefully organize a biblical passage in a systematic way, so that the listeners clearly understand it
   c. instruct on doctrinal topics, to enable the listeners to have a better understanding of these subjects
   d. stress application of passages emphasizing practical truths, so that the listeners can refine their conduct
   e. take one verse and outline practical and specific steps of action for the listener to follow

5. When giving a testimony, he/she tends to:
   a. encourage or console others, rather than just share a verse or experience
   b. indicate some area of doctrine that has come alive through an experience or a shared verse
   c. emphasize the practical application of some verses to his or her life

6. With regard to planning for the future of his/her church, he/she tends to:
   a. have confidence about what the church should do
   b. be more concerned with envisioning end results than with the details involved in getting there

    *c.* have a great desire to see quick growth in the ministries of the church

7. When conversing with other Christians, he/she tends to:
   *a.* probe them to determine their true spiritual condition and needs
   *b.* exhort them to embrace certain goals and actions

8. If a person were to ask him/her to evaluate another's spiritual condition, he/she would tend to:
   *a.* point out errors in the other person's mental understanding of the Christian life
   *b.* sense areas of right and wrong conduct in that person's life, and point out some solutions
   *c.* be critical of areas of that person's life which are not disciplined and well ordered

9. When presented with a physical or spiritual need, he/she tends to:
   *a.* respond on his/her own initiative to try to meet it if possible
   *b.* respond best if someone calls and asks him/her to help
   *c.* not respond if the need requires some time for personal preparation
   *d.* respond with money and possessions

10. In an organization, he/she prefers to (choose only one response):
   *a.* lead a group
   *b.* be a follower under another's leadership

11. When given a task which needs to be done now, he/she tends to:
   *a.* leave it for another task if the second one seems more important at the time
   *b.* be concerned with doing a high quality and thorough job
   *c.* favor doing it himself/herself rather than delegating it

12. If asked to lead somewhere in the church program, he/she would tend to choose a position which involved:
   *a.* detailed planning and decision making for the present
   *b.* harmonizing various viewpoints for a decision

    *c.* evaluating personnel for various leadership
    positions

13. If a group is meeting and no assigned leader is
there, he/she would tend to:
    *a.* assume the leadership
    *b.* let the meeting proceed with no direct
    leadership
    *c.* call someone to find out who the real leader is

14. His/her reaction to the needs of others tends to be:
    *a.* slow, because of not knowing what to do
    *b.* quick, because he/she usually senses what
    needs to be done
    *c.* deliberate, because of wanting to make sure
    he/she has thought it through thoroughly

15. In regard to decision making when the facts are
clear, he/she tends to:
    *a.* lack firmness, because of people's feelings
    *b.* rely on others whom he/she believes are more
    capable of sorting out the issues in the decision

16. With regard to financial matters, he/she tends to:
    *a.* be able to make wise investments and gain
    wealth
    *b.* be moved to give generously to people and
    organizations he/she considers worthy
    *c.* feel deeply that such matters should be handled
    in an orderly and prudent manner
    *d.* see money as a means for carrying out
    ministries and meeting needs, more than for
    construction of buildings, payment of salaries,
    etc.
    *e.* work hard to meet legitimate needs

17. When called upon to serve, he/she is most
naturally motivated to help in situations in which
there are specific:
    *a.* material needs (food, buildings, equipment,
    money)
    *b.* mental needs (lack of understanding of
    Scripture, need to find God's will in a certain
    area, etc.)
    *c.* emotional needs (fear, anxiety, frustration,
    moods due to pain and trials, etc.)
    *d.* spiritual needs (for commitment, faith, dealing
    with sin, etc.)

18. When speaking before people, he/she has the tendency to:
    a. try to persuade people to make spiritual decisions and commitments right then
    b. prepare well and speak carefully
    c. encourage thought-life decisions more than conduct changes
    d. have little interest in emotional commitments unless they are based on clear biblical teaching

OTHERS' ASSESSMENT
OF PREFERENCES AND TENDENCIES
*Instructions:*
A. Circle as many answers to each question as solidly apply to the person you are evaluating. DO NOT LIMIT YOUR RESPONSE TO ONE CHOICE if more than one applies, unless a specific limitation is given along with the question.
B. Circle no response if you find that none of the choices apply. For example, if you believe that the person prefers not to speak or make presentations, do not circle any of the answers in question 4.

1. He/she prefers situations in the church in which he/she is:
   a. a speaker
   b. in a discussion group
   c. just a listener
2. If asked to speak, he/she prefers to speak to:
   a. large groups
   b. small groups
   c. individuals
3. When faced with counseling another person about problems, he/she tends to:
   a. identify deeply with the other person's situation
   b. give the other person the best biblical solution he/she can think of, even if not totally confident about the counsel
   c. prefer sharing biblical insights, avoiding discussions about feelings
   d. urge the person to follow his/her counsel, because he/she honestly believes God helps him/her see the solutions to others' problems
4. When preparing for talks to other Christians,

he/she is normally motivated to:

    *a.* emphasize the truths of basic Bible themes, so as to lead the listeners to a clear-cut decision in the meeting

    *b.* carefully organize a biblical passage in a systematic way, so that the listeners clearly understand it

    *c.* instruct on doctrinal topics, to enable the listeners to have a better understanding of these subjects

    *d.* stress application of passages emphasizing practical truths, so that the listeners can refine their conduct

    *e.* take one verse and outline practical and specific steps of action for the listener to follow

5. When giving a testimony, he/she tends to:

    *a.* encourage or console others, rather than just share a verse or experience

    *b.* indicate some area of doctrine that has come alive to him or her through an experience or a shared verse

    *c.* emphasize the practical application of some verses to his or her life

6. With regard to planning for the future of his/her church, he/she tends to:

    *a.* have confidence about what the church should do

    *b.* be more concerned with envisioning end results than with the details involved in getting there

    *c.* have a great desire to see quick growth in the ministries of the church

7. When conversing with other Christians, he/she tends to:

    *a.* probe them to determine their true spiritual condition and needs

    *b.* exhort them to embrace certain goals and actions

8. If a person were to ask him/her to evaluate another's spiritual condition, he/she would tend to:

    *a.* point out errors in the other person's mental understanding of the Christian life

    *b.* sense areas of right and wrong conduct in that person's life, and point out some solutions

      *c.* be critical of areas of that person's life which
are not disciplined and well ordered

9. When presented with a physical or spiritual need,
he/she tends to:
   - *a.* respond on his/her own initiative to try to meet
it if possible
   - *b.* respond best if someone calls and asks him/her
to help
   - *c.* not respond if the need requires some time for
personal preparation
   - *d.* respond with money and possessions

10. In an organization, he/she prefers to (choose only
one response):
    - *a.* lead a group
    - *b.* be a follower under another's leadership

11. When given a task which needs to be done now,
he/she tends to:
    - *a.* leave it for another task if the second one
seems more important at the time
    - *b.* be concerned with doing a high quality and
thorough job
    - *c.* favor doing it himself/herself rather than
delegating it

12. If asked to lead somewhere in the church
program, he/she would tend to choose a position
which involved:
    - *a.* detailed planning and decision making for the
present
    - *b.* harmonizing various viewpoints for a decision
    - *c.* evaluating personnel for various leadership
positions

13. If a group is meeting and no assigned leader is
there, he/she would tend to:
    - *a.* assume the leadership
    - *b.* let the meeting proceed with no direct
leadership
    - *c.* call someone to find out who the real leader is

14. His/her reaction to the needs of others tends to be:
    - *a.* slow, because of not knowing what to do
    - *b.* quick, because he/she usually senses what
needs to be done
    - *c.* deliberate, because of wanting to make sure
he/she has thought it through thoroughly

15. In regard to decision making when the facts are clear, he/she tends to:
    a. lack firmness, because of people's feelings
    b. rely on others whom he/she believes are more capable of sorting out the issues in the decision
16. With regard to financial matters, he/she tends to:
    a. be able to make wise investments and gain wealth
    b. be moved to give generously to people and organizations he/she considers worthy
    c. feel deeply that such matters should be handled in an orderly and prudent manner
    d. see money as a means for carrying out ministries and meeting needs, more than for construction of buildings, payment of salaries, etc.
    e. work hard to meet legitimate needs
17. When called upon to serve, he/she is most naturally motivated to help in situations in which there are specific:
    a. material needs (food, buildings, equipment, money)
    b. mental needs (lack of understanding of Scripture, need to find God's will in a certain area, etc.)
    c. emotional needs (fear, anxiety, frustration, moods due to pain and trials, etc.)
    d. spiritual needs (for commitment, faith, dealing with sin, etc.)
18. When speaking before people, he/she has the tendency to:
    a. try to persuade people to make spiritual decisions and commitments right then
    b. prepare well and speak carefully
    c. encourage thought-life decisions more than conduct changes
    d. have little interest in emotional commitments unless they are based on clear biblical teaching

OTHERS' ASSESSMENT
OF PREFERENCES AND TENDENCIES
*Instructions:*
  A. Circle as many answers to each question as solidly

apply to the person you are evaluating. DO NOT LIMIT YOUR RESPONSE TO ONE CHOICE if more than one applies, unless a specific limitation is given along with the question.

B. Circle no response if you find that none of the choices apply. For example, if you believe that the person prefers not to speak or make presentations, do not circle any of the answers in question 4.

1. He/she prefers situations in the church in which he/she is:
   a. a speaker
   b. in a discussion group
   c. just a listener

2. If asked to speak, he/she prefers to speak to:
   a. large groups
   b. small groups
   c. individuals

3. When faced with counseling another person about problems, he/she tends to:
   a. identify deeply with the other person's situation
   b. give the other person the best biblical solution he/she can think of, even if not totally confident about the counsel
   c. prefer sharing biblical insights, avoiding discussions about feelings
   d. urge the person to follow his/her counsel, because he/she honestly believes God helps him/her see the solutions to others' problems

4. When preparing for talks to other Christians, he/she is normally motivated to:
   a. emphasize the truths of basic Bible themes, so as to lead the listeners to a clear-cut decision in the meeting
   b. carefully organize a biblical passage in a systematic way, so that the listeners clearly understand it
   c. instruct on doctrinal topics, to enable the listeners to have a better understanding of these subjects
   d. stress application of passages emphasizing practical truths, so that the listeners can refine their conduct

     *e.* take one verse and outline practical and specific steps of action for the listener to follow

5. When giving a testimony, he/she tends to:
     *a.* encourage or console others, rather than just share a verse or experience
     *b.* indicate some area of doctrine that has come alive to him/her through an experience or a shared verse
     *c.* emphasize the practical application of some verses to his or her life

6. With regard to planning for the future of his/her church, he/she tends to:
     *a.* have confidence about what the church should do
     *b.* be more concerned with envisioning end results than with the details involved in getting there
     *c.* have a great desire to see quick growth in the ministries of the church

7. When conversing with other Christians, he/she tends to:
     *a.* probe them to determine their true spiritual condition and needs
     *b.* exhort them to embrace certain goals and actions

8. If a person were to ask him/her to evaluate another's spiritual condition, he/she would tend to:
     *a.* point out errors in the other person's mental understanding of the Christian life
     *b.* sense areas of right and wrong conduct in that person's life, and point out some solutions
     *c.* be critical of areas of that person's life which are not disciplined and well ordered

9. When presented with a physical or spiritual need, he/she tends to:
     *a.* respond on his/her own initiative to try to meet it if possible
     *b.* respond best if someone calls and asks him/her to help
     *c.* not respond if the need requires some time for personal preparation
     *d.* respond with money and possessions

10. In an organization, he/she prefers to (choose only one response):

  *a.* lead a group

  *b.* be a follower under another's leadership

11. When given a task which needs to be done now, he/she tends to:

  *a.* leave it for another task if the second one seems more important at the time

  *b.* be concerned with doing a high quality and thorough job

  *c.* favor doing it himself/herself rather than delegating it

12. If asked to lead somewhere in the church program, he/she would tend to choose a position which involved:

  *a.* detailed planning and decision making for the present

  *b.* harmonizing various viewpoints for a decision

  *c.* evaluating personnel for various leadership positions

13. If a group is meeting and no assigned leader is there, he/she would tend to:

  *a.* assume the leadership

  *b.* let the meeting proceed with no direct leadership

  *c.* call someone to find out who the real leader is

14. His/her reaction to the needs of others tends to be:

  *a.* slow, because of not knowing what to do

  *b.* quick, because he/she usually senses what needs to be done

  *c.* deliberate, because of wanting to make sure he/she has thought it through thoroughly

15. In regard to decision making when the facts are clear, he/she tends to:

  *a.* lack firmness, because of people's feelings

  *b.* rely on others whom he/she believes are more capable of sorting out the issues in the decision

16. With regard to financial matters, he/she tends to:

  *a.* be able to make wise investments and gain wealth

  *b.* be moved to give generously to people and organizations he/she considers worthy

  *c.* feel deeply that such matters should be handled in an orderly and prudent manner

  *d.* see money as a means for carrying out

ministries and meeting needs, more than for
construction of buildings, payment of salaries,
etc.

    *e.* work hard to meet legitimate needs

17. When called upon to serve, he/she is most
naturally motivated to help in situations in which
there are specific:

    *a.* material needs (food, buildings, equipment,
money)

    *b.* mental needs (lack of understanding of
Scripture, need to find God's will in a certain
area, etc.)

    *c.* emotional needs (fear, anxiety, frustration,
moods due to pain and trials, etc.)

    *d.* spiritual needs (for commitment, faith, dealing
with sin, etc.)

18. When speaking before people, he/she has the
tendency to:

    *a.* try to persuade people to make spiritual
decisions and commitments right then

    *b.* prepare well and speak carefully

    *c.* encourage thought-life decisions more than
conduct changes

    *d.* have little interest in emotional commitments
unless they are based on clear biblical teaching

## OTHERS' ASSESSMENT
## OF PREFERENCES AND TENDENCIES

*Instructions:*

A. Circle as many answers to each question as solidly
apply to the person you are evaluating. DO NOT LIMIT
YOUR RESPONSE TO ONE CHOICE if more than one applies,
unless a specific limitation is given along with the
question.

B. Circle no response if you find that none of the choices
apply. For example, if you believe that the person
prefers not to speak or make presentations, do not
circle any of the answers in question 4.

1. He/she prefers situations in the church in which
he/she is:

    *a.* a speaker

    *b.* in a discussion group

    *c.* just a listener

   *2.* If asked to speak, he/she prefers to speak to:

     *a.* large groups

     *b.* small groups

     *c.* individuals

   *3.* When faced with counseling another person about problems, he/she tends to:

     *a.* identify deeply with the other person's situation

     *b.* give the other person the best biblical solution he/she can think of, even if not totally confident about the counsel

     *c.* prefer sharing biblical insights, avoiding discussions about feelings

     *d.* urge the person to follow his/her counsel, because he/she honestly believes God helps him/her see the solutions to others' problems

   *4.* When preparing for talks to other Christians, he/she is normally motivated to:

     *a.* emphasize the truths of basic Bible themes, so as to lead the listeners to a clear-cut decision in the meeting

     *b.* carefully organize a biblical passage in a systematic way, so that the listeners clearly understand it

     *c.* instruct on doctrinal topics, to enable the listeners to have a better understanding of these subjects

     *d.* stress application of passages emphasizing practical truths, so that the listeners can refine their conduct

     *e.* take one verse and outline practical and specific steps of action for the listener to follow

   *5.* When giving a testimony, he/she tends to:

     *a.* encourage or console others, rather than just share a verse or experience

     *b.* indicate some area of doctrine that has come alive to him/her through an experience or a shared verse

     *c.* emphasize the practical application of some verses to his or her life

   *6.* With regard to planning for the future of his/her church, he/she tends to:

     *a.* have confidence about what the church should do

      *b.* be more concerned with envisioning end results than with the details involved in getting there

      *c.* have a great desire to see quick growth in the ministries of the church

7. When conversing with other Christians, he/she tends to:

      *a.* probe them to determine their true spiritual condition and needs

      *b.* exhort them to embrace certain goals and actions

8. If a person were to ask him/her to evaluate another's spiritual condition, he/she would tend to:

      *a.* point out errors in the other person's mental understanding of the Christian life

      *b.* sense areas of right and wrong conduct in that person's life, and point out some solutions

      *c.* be critical of areas of that person's life which are not disciplined and well ordered

9. When presented with a physical or spiritual need, he/she tends to:

      *a.* respond on his/her own initiative to try to meet it if possible

      *b.* respond best if someone calls and asks him/her to help

      *c.* not respond if the need requires some time for personal preparation

      *d.* respond with money and possessions

10. In an organization, he/she prefers to (choose only one response):

      *a.* lead a group

      *b.* be a follower under another's leadership

11. When given a task which needs to be done now, he/she tends to:

      *a.* leave it for another task if the second one seems more important at the time

      *b.* be concerned with doing a high quality and thorough job

      *c.* favor doing it himself/herself rather than delegating it

12. If asked to lead somewhere in the church program, he/she would tend to choose a position which involved:

    *a.* detailed planning and decision making for the present
    *b.* harmonizing various viewpoints for a decision
    *c.* evaluating personnel for various leadership positions

13. If a group is meeting and no assigned leader is there, he/she would tend to:
    *a.* assume the leadership
    *b.* let the meeting proceed with no direct leadership
    *c.* call someone to find out who the real leader is

14. His/her reaction to the needs of others tends to be:
    *a.* slow, because of not knowing what to do
    *b.* quick, because he/she usually senses what needs to be done
    *c.* deliberate, because of wanting to make sure he/she has thought it through thoroughly

15. In regard to decision making when the facts are clear, he/she tends to:
    *a.* lack firmness, because of people's feelings
    *b.* rely on others whom he/she believes are more capable of sorting out the issues in the decision

16. With regard to financial matters, he/she tends to:
    *a.* be able to make wise investments and gain wealth
    *b.* be moved to give generously to people and organizations he/she considers worthy
    *c.* feel deeply that such matters should be handled in an orderly and prudent manner
    *d.* see money as a means for carrying out ministries and meeting needs, more than for construction of buildings, payment of salaries, etc.
    *e.* work hard to meet legitimate needs

17. When called upon to serve, he/she is most naturally motivated to help in situations in which there are specific:
    *a.* material needs (food, buildings, equipment, money)
    *b.* mental needs (lack of understanding of Scripture, need to find God's will in a certain area, etc.)
    *c.* emotional needs (fear, anxiety, frustration, moods due to pain and trials, etc.)
    *d.* spiritual needs (for commitment, faith, dealing with sin, etc.)

*18.* When speaking before people, he/she has the
tendency to:
  *a.* try to persuade people to make spiritual
    decisions and commitments right then
  *b.* prepare well and speak carefully
  *c.* encourage thought-life decisions more than
    conduct changes
  *d.* have little interest in emotional commitments
    unless they are based on clear biblical teaching

## SCORE SHEET FOR OTHERS' ASSESSMENT OF PREFERENCES AND TENDENCIES

*Instructions:*

1. In the far left-hand column of this score sheet is a list
   of all the possible responses for the multiple choice
   questionnaire (1a, 1b, 1c, etc.). Transfer the circled
   answers from the questionnaire to this score sheet by
   circling each answer in the left-hand column that you
   find circled in the questionnaire.
2. Each circled answer indicates a preference for one or
   more spiritual gifts. The spiritual gifts preferred by a
   given answer are indicated by an X in the boxes to
   the right of the response. For example, if you find
   circled the answer 1a in the questionnaire, it
   indicates that you prefer preaching, teaching, and
   ruling, since the X's in the boxes to the right of 1a
   fall in the columns for those gifts.
3. Circle every X that you see as you move from the
   circled answers at the left across the page to your
   right. Do this for each circled response in the
   left-hand column.
4. Now, go to the end of the score sheet and notice that
   you must enter the total number of circled X's for
   each gift. To do this, count the circled X's in each gift
   column and enter the total in the box provided.
5. Then, go to the percentage equivalent chart at the
   end of the score sheet. Find the percentage equivalent
   to the number circled and enter it in the "% CIRCLED
   box" below the "TOTAL CIRCLED" box.
6. The top three or four percentages will indicate the
   gifts toward which you seem to show the greatest
   preference or tendency.
7. Follow the procedures 1—6 above for each of the four

questionnaires completed by others. Evaluate the four score sheets and enter the top three or four gifts on page 78, under 2.

8. See Appendix III if you have difficulty scoring the questionnaires.

| | PREACHING | TEACHING | KNOWLEDGE | WISDOM | EXHORTATION | FAITH | DISCERNMENT OF SPIRITS | HELPS | SERVING | ADMINISTRATION | RULING | MERCY | GIVING |
|---|---|---|---|---|---|---|---|---|---|---|---|---|---|
| 1a | X | X | | | | | | | | | X | | |
| 1b | | X | X | X | X | X | X | | | X | | | |
| 1c | | | | | | | | | | | | X | |
| 2a | X | X | | | X | | | | | | | | |
| 2b | | X | X | X | | X | X | | | X | | | |
| 2c | | | | | X | | | X | | | | X | |
| 3a | | | | | X | | | X | X | | | X | X |
| 3b | X | X | | | X | | | | | | X | X | |
| 3c | | X | | | | | | | | | | | |
| 3d | | | | X | X | | X | | | | | | |
| 4a | X | | | | | | | | | | | | |
| 4b | | X | | | | | | | | | | | |
| 4c | | | X | | | | | | | | | | |
| 4d | | | | X | | | | | | | | | |
| 4e | | | | | X | | | | | | | | |
| 5a | | | | X | X | | | | | | | X | |
| 5b | X | X | X | | | | | | | | | | |
| 5c | X | | | | X | | | X | X | X | | | |
| 6a | | | | | X | | | | | | | | |
| 6b | | | | | X | | | | | | | | |
| 6c | | | | | X | | | | | | | | |
| 7a | | | | | | X | | | | | | | |
| 7b | | | | | X | X | | | | | | | |
| 8a | X | X | X | | | | | | | | | | |
| 8b | | | | | X | X | | | | | | | |
| 8c | | | | | | | | | | X | X | | |
| 9a | | | | | | | | | X | | | | X |
| 9b | | | | | | | | X | | | | | |
| 9c | | | | | | | | X | | | | | |

| | PREACHING | TEACHING | KNOWLEDGE | WISDOM | EXHORTATION | FAITH | DISCERNMENT OF SPIRITS | HELPS | SERVING | ADMINISTRATION | RULING | MERCY | GIVING |
|---|---|---|---|---|---|---|---|---|---|---|---|---|---|
| 9d | | | | | | | | | | | | | X |
| 10a | X | | | | | | | | X | X | X | | |
| 10b | | | | | | | | X | | | | X | |
| 11a | | | | | | | | | X | | | | |
| 11b | | | | | | | | | X | X | X | | |
| 11c | | | | | | | | X | X | | | X | X |
| 12a | | | | | | | | | | X | | | |
| 12b | | | | | | | | | | X | X | | |
| 12c | | | | | | | X | | | | | | |
| 13a | | | | | | | | | X | | X | | |
| 13b | | | | | | | | X | | | | | |
| 13c | | | | X | | | | | | | | | |
| 14a | | | X | | | | | | | | | | |
| 14b | | | | | X | X | | | X | | | X | X |
| 14c | | | X | | | | X | | | X | X | | |
| 15a | | | | | | | | | | | | X | |
| 15b | | | | | | | | X | | | | | |
| 16a | | | | | | | | | | | | | X |
| 16b | | | | | | | | | | | | | X |
| 16c | | | | | | | | | | X | X | | X |
| 16d | | | | | | X | | | | | | | |
| 16e | | | | | | | | | | | | | X |
| 17a | | | | | | | | X | X | X | X | | X |
| 17b | | X | X | X | | | | | | | | | |
| 17c | | | | | X | | | | | | | X | |
| 17d | X | | | | | X | X | | | | | | |
| 18a | X | | | | | | | | | | | | |
| 18b | | X | | | | | | | | | | | |
| 18c | | | X | | | | | | | | | | |
| 18d | | | X | | | | | | | | | | |

TOTAL
CIRCLED

CIRCLED

69

PERCENTAGES

| | Total Circled | % | Total Circled | % |
|---|---|---|---|---|
| | 1 | 10 | 6 | 60 |
| | 2 | 20 | 7 | 70 |
| | 3 | 30 | 8 | 80 |
| | 4 | 40 | 9 | 90 |
| | 5 | 50 | 10 | 100 |

| | PREACHING | TEACHING | KNOWLEDGE | WISDOM | EXHORTATION | FAITH | DISCERNMENT OF SPIRITS | HELPS | SERVING | ADMINISTRATION | RULING | MERCY | GIVING |
|---|---|---|---|---|---|---|---|---|---|---|---|---|---|
| 1a | X | X | | | | | | | | | X | | |
| 1b | | X | X | X | X | X | X | | | X | | | |
| 1c | | | | | | | | | | | | X | |
| 2a | X | X | | | X | | | | | | | | |
| 2b | | X | X | X | | X | X | | | X | | | |
| 2c | | | | X | | | | X | | | | X | |
| 3a | | | | | X | | | X | X | | | X | X |
| 3b | X | X | | | | X | | | | | X | X | |
| 3c | | X | | | | | | | | | | | |
| 3d | | | | X | X | | X | | | | | | |
| 4a | X | | | | | | | | | | | | |
| 4b | | X | | | | | | | | | | | |
| 4c | | | X | | | | | | | | | | |
| 4d | | | | X | | | | | | | | | |
| 4e | | | | | X | | | | | | | | |
| 5a | | | | X | X | | | | | | | X | |
| 5b | X | X | X | | | | | | | | | | |
| 5c | X | | | X | | | X | X | X | | | | |
| 6a | | | | | X | | | | | | | | |
| 6b | | | | | X | | | | | | | | |
| 6c | | | | | X | | | | | | | | |
| 7a | | | | | | X | | | | | | | |
| 7b | | | | | X | X | | | | | | | |
| 8a | X | X | X | | | | | | | | | | |
| 8b | | | | | X | X | | | | | | | |
| 8c | | | | | | | | | | X | X | | |
| 9a | | | | | | | | | X | | | | X |
| 9b | | | | | | | | X | | | | | |
| 9c | | | | | | | | X | | | | | |

| PREACHING | TEACHING | KNOWLEDGE | WISDOM | EXHORTATION | FAITH | DISCERNMENT OF SPIRITS | HELPS | SERVING | ADMINISTRATION | RULING | MERCY | GIVING | |
|---|---|---|---|---|---|---|---|---|---|---|---|---|---|
| | | | | | | | | | | | | X | 9d |
| X | | | | | | | | X | X | X | | | 10a |
| | | | | | | | X | | | | X | | 10b |
| | | | | | | | | X | | | | | 11a |
| | | | | | | | | X | X | X | | | 11b |
| | | | | | | | X | X | | | X | X | 11c |
| | | | | | | | | | X | | | | 12a |
| | | | | | | | | | X | X | | | 12b |
| | | | | | | X | | | | | | | 12c |
| | | | | | | | | X | | X | | | 13a |
| | | | | | | | X | | | | | | 13b |
| | | | X | | | | | | | | | | 13c |
| | | X | | | | | | | | | | | 14a |
| | | | | X | X | | | X | | | X | X | 14b |
| | | X | | | | X | | | X | X | | | 14c |
| | | | | | | | | | | | X | | 15a |
| | | | | | | | X | | | | | | 15b |
| | | | | | | | | | | | | X | 16a |
| | | | | | | | | | | | | X | 16b |
| | | | | | | | | | X | X | | X | 16c |
| | | | | | X | | | | | | | | 16d |
| | | | | | | | | | | | | X | 16e |
| | | | | | | | | X | X | X | | X | 17a |
| | X | X | X | | | | | | | | | | 17b |
| | | | | X | | | | | | | X | | 17c |
| X | | | | | X | X | | | | | | | 17d |
| X | | | | | | | | | | | | | 18a |
| | X | | | | | | | | | | | | 18b |
| | | X | | | | | | | | | | | 18c |
| | | X | | | | | | | | | | | 18d |
| | | | | | | | | | | | | | |
| | | | | | | | | | | | | | TOTAL CIRCLED |
| | | | | | | | | | | | | | % CIRCLED |

71

| | Total Circled | % | Total Circled | % |
|---|---|---|---|---|
| PERCENTAGES | 1 | 10 | 6 | 60 |
| | 2 | 20 | 7 | 70 |
| | 3 | 30 | 8 | 80 |
| | 4 | 40 | 9 | 90 |
| | 5 | 50 | 10 | 100 |

| | PREACHING | TEACHING | KNOWLEDGE | WISDOM | EXHORTATION | FAITH | DISCERNMENT OF SPIRITS | HELPS | SERVING | ADMINISTRATION | RULING | MERCY | GIVING |
|---|---|---|---|---|---|---|---|---|---|---|---|---|---|
| 1a | X | X | | | | | | | | | X | | |
| 1b | | X | X | X | X | X | X | | | X | | | |
| 1c | | | | | | | | | | | | X | |
| 2a | X | X | | | X | | | | | | | | |
| 2b | | X | X | X | | X | X | | | X | | | |
| 2c | | | | X | | | | X | | | | X | |
| 3a | | | | X | | | | X | X | | | X | X |
| 3b | X | X | | | | X | | | | | X | X | |
| 3c | | | X | | | | | | | | | | |
| 3d | | | | | X | X | | X | | | | | |
| 4a | X | | | | | | | | | | | | |
| 4b | | X | | | | | | | | | | | |
| 4c | | | X | | | | | | | | | | |
| 4d | | | | | X | | | | | | | | |
| 4e | | | | | X | | | | | | | | |
| 5a | | | | | X | X | | | | | | X | |
| 5b | X | X | X | | | | | | | | | | |
| 5c | X | | | | X | | | X | X | X | | | |
| 6a | | | | | X | | | | | | | | |
| 6b | | | | | X | | | | | | | | |
| 6c | | | | | X | | | | | | | | |
| 7a | | | | | | X | | | | | | | |
| 7b | | | | | X | X | | | | | | | |
| 8a | X | X | X | | | | | | | | | | |
| 8b | | | | | X | X | | | | | | | |
| 8c | | | | | | | | | | | X | X | |
| 9a | | | | | | | | | | X | | | X |
| 9b | | | | | | | | X | | | | | |
| 9c | | | | | | | | X | | | | | |

| PREACHING | TEACHING | KNOWLEDGE | WISDOM | EXHORTATION | FAITH | DISCERNMENT OF SPIRITS | HELPS | SERVING | ADMINISTRATION | RULING | MERCY | GIVING | |
|---|---|---|---|---|---|---|---|---|---|---|---|---|---|
| | | | | | | | | | | | | X | 9d |
| X | | | | | | | | X | X | X | | | 10a |
| | | | | | | | X | | | | X | | 10b |
| | | | | | | | | X | | | | | 11a |
| | | | | | | | | X | X | X | | | 11b |
| | | | | | | | X | X | | | X | X | 11c |
| | | | | | | | | | X | | | | 12a |
| | | | | | | | | X | X | | | | 12b |
| | | | | | | X | | | | | | | 12c |
| | | | | | | | | X | | X | | | 13a |
| | | | | | | | X | | | | | | 13b |
| | | | X | | | | | | | | | | 13c |
| | | X | | | | | | | | | | | 14a |
| | | | X | X | | | | X | | | X | X | 14b |
| | | X | | | | X | | | X | X | | | 14c |
| | | | | | | | | | | | X | | 15a |
| | | | | | | | X | | | | | | 15b |
| | | | | | | | | | | | | X | 16a |
| | | | | | | | | | | | | X | 16b |
| | | | | | | | | | X | X | | X | 16c |
| | | | | X | | | | | | | | | 16d |
| | | | | | | | | | | | | X | 16e |
| | | | | | | | X | X | X | X | | X | 17a |
| | X | X | X | | | | | | | | | | 17b |
| | | | X | | | | | | | | X | | 17c |
| X | | | | | X | X | | | | | | | 17d |
| X | | | | | | | | | | | | | 18a |
| | X | | | | | | | | | | | | 18b |
| | | X | | | | | | | | | | | 18c |
| | | X | | | | | | | | | | | 18d |
| | | | | | | | | | | | | | |
| | | | | | | | | | | | | | TOTAL CIRCLED |
| | | | | | | | | | | | | | CIRCLED |

| | Total Circled | % | Total Circled | % |
|---|---|---|---|---|
| | 1 | 10 | 6 | 60 |
| | 2 | 20 | 7 | 70 |
| | 3 | 30 | 8 | 80 |
| | 4 | 40 | 9 | 90 |
| | 5 | 50 | 10 | 100 |

| | PREACHING | TEACHING | KNOWLEDGE | WISDOM | EXHORTATION | FAITH | DISCERNMENT OF SPIRITS | HELPS | SERVING | ADMINISTRATION | RULING | MERCY | GIVING |
|---|---|---|---|---|---|---|---|---|---|---|---|---|---|
| 1a | X | X | | | | | | | | | X | | |
| 1b | | X | X | X | X | X | X | | | X | | | |
| 1c | | | | | | | | | | | | X | |
| 2a | X | X | | | X | | | | | | | | |
| 2b | | X | X | X | | X | X | | | X | | | |
| 2c | | | | X | | | | X | | | | X | |
| 3a | | | | | X | | | X | X | | | X | X |
| 3b | X | X | | | X | | | | | | X | X | |
| 3c | | | X | | | | | | | | | | |
| 3d | | | | X | X | | X | | | | | | |
| 4a | X | | | | | | | | | | | | |
| 4b | | X | | | | | | | | | | | |
| 4c | | | X | | | | | | | | | | |
| 4d | | | | X | | | | | | | | | |
| 4e | | | | | X | | | | | | | | |
| 5a | | | | X | X | | | | | | | X | |
| 5b | X | X | X | | | | | | | | | | |
| 5c | X | | | | X | | X | X | X | | | | |
| 6a | | | | | X | | | | | | | | |
| 6b | | | | | X | | | | | | | | |
| 6c | | | | | X | | | | | | | | |
| 7a | | | | | | X | | | | | | | |
| 7b | | | | | X | X | | | | | | | |
| 8a | X | X | X | | | | | | | | | | |
| 8b | | | | | X | X | | | | | | | |
| 8c | | | | | | | | | | | X | X | |
| 9a | | | | | | | | | | X | | | X |
| 9b | | | | | | | | X | | | | | |
| 9c | | | | | | | | X | | | | | |

| PREACHING | TEACHING | KNOWLEDGE | WISDOM | EXHORTATION | FAITH | DISCERNMENT OF SPIRITS | HELPS | SERVING | ADMINISTRATION | RULING | MERCY | GIVING | |
|---|---|---|---|---|---|---|---|---|---|---|---|---|---|
| | | | | | | | | | | | | X | 9d |
| X | | | | | | | | X | X | X | | | 10a |
| | | | | | | | X | | | | X | | 10b |
| | | | | | | | | X | | | | | 11a |
| | | | | | | | | X | X | X | | | 11b |
| | | | | | | | X | X | | | X | X | 11c |
| | | | | | | | | | X | | | | 12a |
| | | | | | | | | | X | X | | | 12b |
| | | | | | | X | | | | | | | 12c |
| | | | | | | | | X | | X | | | 13a |
| | | | | | | | X | | | | | | 13b |
| | | | X | | | | | | | | | | 13c |
| | | X | | | | | | | | | | | 14a |
| | | | | X | X | | | X | | | X | X | 14b |
| | | | X | | | X | | | X | X | | | 14c |
| | | | | | | | | | | | X | | 15a |
| | | | | | | | X | | | | | | 15b |
| | | | | | | | | | | | | X | 16a |
| | | | | | | | | | | | | X | 16b |
| | | | | | | | | | X | X | | X | 16c |
| | | | | | X | | | | | | | | 16d |
| | | | | | | | | | | | | X | 16e |
| | | | | | | | X | X | X | X | | X | 17a |
| | X | X | X | | | | | | | | | | 17b |
| | | | | X | | | | | | | X | | 17c |
| X | | | | | X | X | | | | | | | 17d |
| X | | | | | | | | | | | | | 18a |
| | X | | | | | | | | | | | | 18b |
| | | X | | | | | | | | | | | 18c |
| | | X | | | | | | | | | | | 18d |
| | | | | | | | | | | | | | TOTAL CIRCLED |
| | | | | | | | | | | | | | CIRCLED |

| | Total Circled | % | Total Circled | % |
|---|---|---|---|---|
| PERCENTAGES | 1 | 10 | 6 | 60 |
| | 2 | 20 | 7 | 70 |
| | 3 | 30 | 8 | 80 |
| | 4 | 40 | 9 | 90 |
| | 5 | 50 | 10 | 100 |

# EIGHT
## Evaluation Three:
## Past Christian Service Experiences

*Instructions:*
A. List below the areas of church ministry in which you
have served in the past; evaluate them according to
the categories given. Place a check mark on the line
below high, average, or low evaluation for each area
of service and for each method of evaluation.

| Areas of service | Degree of motivation to do the task | | | Sense of personal accomplishment | | | Fruits which resulted | | |
|---|---|---|---|---|---|---|---|---|---|
| | *high* | *avg.* | *low* | *high* | *avg.* | *low* | *high* | *avg.* | *low* |
| _____ | ___ | ___ | ___ | ___ | ___ | ___ | ___ | ___ | ___ |
| _____ | ___ | ___ | ___ | ___ | ___ | ___ | ___ | ___ | ___ |
| _____ | ___ | ___ | ___ | ___ | ___ | ___ | ___ | ___ | ___ |
| _____ | ___ | ___ | ___ | ___ | ___ | ___ | ___ | ___ | ___ |
| _____ | ___ | ___ | ___ | ___ | ___ | ___ | ___ | ___ | ___ |
| _____ | ___ | ___ | ___ | ___ | ___ | ___ | ___ | ___ | ___ |
| _____ | ___ | ___ | ___ | ___ | ___ | ___ | ___ | ___ | ___ |

B. In connection with the above evaluations, were there
any special circumstances which affected your
response that would not be true of a normal situation?
If so, explain.

_____

_____

_____

C. Based upon the assessments in evaluations 1 and 2
above, and upon your understanding of the spiritual
gifts already studied, turn to page 78 and complete
3.

## SUMMARY OF PERSONAL EVALUATIONS
1. Based on my assessment of my preferences using the
multiple choice indicator, I appear to have one of the
following gifts:
   a._____
   b._____
   c._____
   d._____
   e._____

2. Based on others' assessment of my preferences, I appear to have one of the following gifts:

   *a.*_____

   *b.*_____

   *c.*_____

   *d.*_____

   *e.*_____

3. Based on my evaluation of past Christian experiences, I appear to have which of the following gifts listed in either 1 or 2 above?

   *a.*_____

   *b.*_____

   *c.*_____

   *d.*_____

   *e.*_____

# NINE
# Evaluating Yourself
# Against Each Gift

Through the foregoing study of spiritual gifts and the several evaluations of your own preferences and tendencies, you now have a basis upon which to make a final evaluation of your possible gift(s). As you think through the following summaries of the thirteen spiritual gifts, look for the one or more most closely aligned with your evaluations. Be praying that God will give you true wisdom in this judgment.

*Instructions:*
  A. Using the evaluations of your preferences and past experiences, analyze the following definitions of the gifts with a view to determining which one(s) you might have.
  B. Under the evaluation section for each gift, complete the sentence by underlining either *(may)* or *(may not)*, and by giving the reason for your conclusion.
  C. Summarize your conclusions at the end of this chapter.

*Descriptions of each gift*

## I. SPEAKING GIFTS
  A. Prophecy—the God-given ability to take the truth of God in the Bible and speak it forth with the result that lives are changed (see Romans 12:6).
  Tendencies of a person with this gift:
  1. Prefers speaking to groups over individual interaction
  2. Carefully studies Scripture before speaking
  3. Exhorts, teaches, and consoles in his/her messages, rather than doing just one of these three.
  4. Urges others to make big decisions immediately, rather than working for long-range, small changes in behavior
  5. May have difficulty in being sensitive to and patient with individuals' problems
  Evaluation: I *(may)* *(may not)* have this gift because

  B. Teaching—the God-given ability to systematically and

effectively organize and explain the principles of the Bible (see Romans 12:7).

Tendencies of a person with this gift:

1. Relies definitely and assuredly on the authority of the Scriptures
2. Delights in research and systematic presentation of truth
3. Is tenacious about keeping verses in context and being accurate in every statement made
4. Prefers a public ministry (for which he/she can prepare) to individual counseling
5. Tends to be critical of others with different positions on biblical doctrine
6. Has a balanced emphasis on logic, word meanings, and practical application for life changes

Evaluation: I *(may) (may not)* have this gift because

_____

_____

C. Word of knowledge—the God-given ability to translate and interpret biblical truth for preaching and teaching (see 1 Corinthians 12:8).

Tendencies of a person with this gift:

1. Has interest in and places emphasis on the doctrines of Scripture, i.e., nature of God, God's eternal plans, etc., and mentally grasps the way these pieces of knowledge fit into the whole of doctrine.
2. Shows ability to understand and remember doctrine; may tend to measure the degree of spiritual maturity in others mainly by the amount of biblical knowledge they retain
3. Emphasizes knowledge in a passage more than its life-relatedness
4. Finds practical applications of Scripture and counseling to be difficult tasks

Evaluation: I *(may) (may not)* have this gift because

_____

_____

D. Word of wisdom—the God-given ability to take the knowledge of God's Word and apply it by principles and insights to practical living (see 1 Corinthians 12:8).

Tendencies of a person with this gift:
1. Has interest in biblical truth as it applies to conduct
2. Emphasizes the more practical portions of Scripture for study
3. Places careful emphasis on attaining insight regarding the Lord's will
4. Has no intense interest in (and may question the value of) in-depth doctrinal studies
5. Is suspicious of all nonbiblical insights from life and the social sciences, because of unique appreciation for the scriptural perspective
6. Will tend more toward unifying people than causing division based on doctrinal differences

Evaluation: I *(may)* *(may not)* have this gift because

_____

_____

E. Exhortation—the God-given ability to come alongside others to encourage, counsel, and console them, using the Scriptures (see Romans 12:8).
Tendencies of a person with this gift:
1. Identifies emotionally and mentally with others in their predicaments
2. Visualizes goals and steps of action for others to follow
3. Appeals to the will by asking, urging, and requesting certain courses of action publicly
4. Speaks with a sense of urgency, appearing at times to oversimplify problems because of confidence in steps of action prescribed
5. May have personal struggles with studying the Scriptures in depth because of greater concern for practical applications from surface reading
6. May use the Scriptures more to support or illustrate his/her practical insight, than as the base from which true interpretation and application come

Evaluation: I *(may)* *(may not)* have this gift because

_____

_____

## II. SERVING GIFTS
A. Faith—the God-given ability to exercise

wonder-working faith, to see beyond the problems and needs to the resource, God (see 1 Corinthians 12:9).
Tendencies of a person with this gift:

1. Has a strong belief in and reliance on God when foresight and future goals are involved
2. Desires to see seemingly impossible tasks accomplished
3. Provides continual vision for others amid seemingly hopeless situations
4. Has feelings of impatience with logical, cautious thinkers
5. Is concerned with end goals and tends to overlook details, considering them unimportant
6. Is usually not responsive to counsel and refinements of his/her goals

Evaluation: I *(may) (may not)* have this gift because

_____

_____

B. Discernment of spirits—the God-given ability to differentiate between the sources of man's speech and actions, whether from the Holy Spirit or from some other spirit (see 1 Corinthians 12:10).
Tendencies of a person with this gift:

1. Gives in to his impulse to probe people in order to ascertain their true spiritual character
2. Is quick to analyze the reasonings and rationalizations of others
3. Has profound sense of right and wrong
4. Assists others in identifying root spiritual problems
5. Has a tendency to render judgments on people's spiritual condition, and thus avoids helping them to see the needed process of change

Evaluation: I *(may) (may not)* have this gift because

_____

_____

C. Helps—the God-given ability to be willing and available to help out in any area in which there is a need (see 1 Corinthians 12:28).
Tendencies of a person with this gift:

1. Is deeply impressed with biblical exhortations to serve other Christians
2. Is sensitive to meeting the immediate needs of

people when called upon or when any need(s) come to his/her attention

3. Does not seek a leadership position, but seeks to serve under someone else
4. Prefers to respond to a need which does not require preparation time and organizational detail
5. Does not emphasize finishing tasks or verbally witnessing for Christ

Evaluation: I *(may) (may not)* have this gift because

_____

_____

D. Serving—the God-given ability to meet the needs, especially the material needs, of others (see Romans 12:7).
   Tendencies of a person with this gift:
   1. Is self-motivated to serve others and meet their immediate needs without others' leadership; frustrated by long-range goals of any kind
   2. Visualizes fulfillment of practical needs of people as opposed to deeper spiritual needs
   3. Has a tendency to overinvolvement because of sensitivity to practical needs of people in the church; personal priorities may suffer
   4. Desires tasks to be done with high quality and enthusiasm
   5. May appear pushy and irritated by policies and red tape, due to desire to get things done

Evaluation: I *(may) (may not)* have this gift because

_____

_____

E. Administration—the God-given ability to guide and direct the workings of the church with skill (see 1 Corinthians 12:4).
   Tendencies of a person with this gift:
   1. Aspires to positions which require charting courses of action and decision making
   2. Is conscious of efficiency and order (or lack of order) within the church
   3. Can carry on discussions, summarize, draw conclusions, and often harmonize the best from various points of view
   4. Has a tendency to be so convinced of his/her own

opinions that he/she stifles discussion and resents opposition

Evaluation: I *(may) (may not)* have this gift because

_____

_____

F. Ruling—the God-given ability to stand before others to preside and effectively lead others with care and diligence (see Romans 12:8).
Tendencies of a person with this gift:
1. Has a compulsion for church business to be done in an orderly fashion, and inwardly reacts with strong feelings toward inadequate procedures
2. Has ability and interest in learning to lead
3. Is more naturally concerned with overall organizational objectives and programs than with the feelings and individual spiritual needs of others
4. May desire and actually carry out a thorough job of leading Bible studies
5. Tends to assume leadership, organize, and delegate responsibilities if no assigned leader exists in a group

Evaluation: I *(may) (may not)* have this gift because

_____

_____

G. Mercy—the God-given ability to show compassion for the misery of others and to relieve the problem with a true attitude of cheerfulness (see Romans 12:8).
Tendencies of a person with this gift:
1. Is cheerful, noncondemning, compassionate, and sensitive to others' distresses
2. Is quick to respond to others' needs for help
3. Attracts those with inward struggles because he/she is sympathetic, conveying an air of understanding
4. Lacks firmness and decisiveness since he/she is so sensitive toward possibly offending others
5. Resents others who are not as sensitive as he/she is to personal needs

Evaluation: I *(may) (may not)* have this gift because

_____

_____

H. Giving—the God-given ability to give liberally with love and joy (see Romans 12:8).

Tendencies of a person with this gift:
1. Is sensitive to the material needs of others and desires to meet those needs without publicity
2. Is always ready to give; can make quick decisions regarding helping others in their needs
3. Has the ability to gain wealth and make wise investments
4. Works hard in order to have enough to share with others; keeps that goal in his/her mind rather than only adding to personal wealth
5. May measure the spiritual maturity of others by the percentage of income or the absolute amount they give to the church and Christian organizations

Evaluation: I *(may) (may not)* have this gift because

_____

_____

CONCLUSION. As a result of this evaluation and in conjunction with the other evaluations, I believe I may have one of the following spiritual gifts:

1. _____
2. _____
3. _____
4. _____
5. _____

# TEN
# Making
# a Commitment

Now that you have determined the possible areas of your spiritual gift, you can test whether or not you have a given gift by serving. The following partial list of church ministry opportunities is classified according to spiritual gifts. The abilities necessary to accomplish these tasks are often found in those with the spiritual gift listed. Prayerfully determine the top three or four gifts you want to test; then, go through the list of ministries under each of the gifts you are interested in testing. Check those you would consider tackling.

## Preaching

boards and commissions
  elder
  deacon
  evangelism

Bible teacher
  migrant worker
  prisons
  hospitals
  rest homes

military

pastor

missionary
  church planting
  evangelism

gospel teams
  evangelistic services
   speaker

## Teaching

boards and commissions
  elder
  deacon
  Christian education

church services
  toddler church
  beginner church
  primary church

home visitation

young people
  Pioneer Girls
  King's Sons
  Christian Service
   Brigade

Boy Scouts
Girl Scouts

outreach
  gospel team
  small group home Bible
   study leader

Sunday school
  superintendent
  assistant superintendent
  department coordinator
  children's teacher
  youth teacher
  adult teacher
  substitute teacher

vacation Bible school
  committee
  teacher
  assistant

missionary-teacher

international student
  ministry
    teacher

## *Knowledge*

boards and commissions
  elder
  deacon
  Christian education

young people
  Pioneer Girls
  King's Sons
  Christian Service
    Brigade
  Boy Scouts
  Girl Scouts

outreach
  small group home Bible
    study discussion leader

Sunday school
  superintendent
  assistant superintendent
  youth teacher
  adult teacher

vacation Bible school
  teacher

missionary
  translation
  interpretation—com-
    mentaries

research
  Sunday school
    curriculum
  Bible school curriculum

## *Wisdom*

boards and commissions
  elder
  deacon
  trustee
  school commission
  building commission
  finance commission

librarian

outreach
  home visitation
  small group home Bible
    study leader
  gospel teams

young people

youth sponsors
Pioneer Girls
King's Sons
Christian Service
  Brigade
Boy Scouts
Girl Scouts
teen week speaker

counseling
  vocational
  minority group
    programs
  gang ministries
  marriage
  homosexuals

divorced
released prisoners
widows and widowers

missionary
planning

church planting
school instruction

vacation Bible school
director

## Exhortation

boards and commissions
elder
deacon
Christian education

Church services
toddler
beginner
primary
adult
vocal music
usher
greeter

visitation
sick
newcomers
shut-ins
canvassing
members
prison
hospital
rest homes
telephone

young people
Pioneer Girls
King's Sons

Christian Service
Brigade
Boy Scouts
Girl Scouts

outreach
gospel teams

counselor
emotionally disturbed
divorced
premarital
gangs
homosexuals
juvenile offenders
marriage conflicts
narcotic addicts
potential suicides
released prison
offenders
runaway youths
school dropouts
widows and widowers
camp

vacation Bible school
teacher

## Faith

boards and commissions
elder
deacon
trustee

nominating committee
missionary commission
building commission
school commission

outreach
  home visitation
  gospel teams
  evangelism

missionary
  church planting

## Discernment of Spirits

boards and commissions
  elder
  deacon
  membership commission
  Christian education
    commission
  nominating committee
  missionary commission
  school commission

personnel recruitment

outreach
  home visitation

young people
  youth sponsors

counselor
  church
  camp
  juvenile offenders
  marriage conflicts
  divorced
  neglected children
  neglectful parents
  runaway youth
  potential suicide
  school dropouts

librarian
Sunday school
  adult

## Helps

boards and commissions
  deaconess
  social commission
  trustee
  finance commission
  property commission
  school commission
  building commission

officers
  treasurer
  financial secretary
  clerk

church services
  usher
  greeter

librarian

nursery
  coordinator
  assistant

missionary
  women's missionary
    circle leader
  White Cross worker

men's fellowship
  committee

outreach
  gospel teams-trans-
    portation
  Bible school host/hostess
  Home Bible study
    host/hostess

Sunday school
  secretary
  departmental secretary

music
  chancel choir director
  youth choir director
  children's choir director
  song leader
  choir member
  soloist
  trio
  quartet
  duet
  pianist—accompanist
          —soloist
  organist
  instrumentalist
  orchestra leader
  music committee

bus driver

banquet worker

office help
  type
  draw
  file
  assemble
  reproduce materials
  mailings
  telephoning
  record information
  key punching

hospitality
  meals
  lodging

transportation
  shut-ins
  youth activities
  church services

bus driver—conventional
          —diesel

cook

nurse

kitchen help

athletic teams
  basketball
  baseball/softball
  volleyball
  swimming
  football
  other _____

maintenance
  landscaping
  carpentry
  painting
  electrical
  plumbing
  cleaning

artistic work

financial
  accounting
  bookkeeping
  money counting
  computer

audiovisual
  video-taping
  projectionist
  filing
  printer/posters
  television
  photographer
  artist
  tape recorder

Sunday school
  hear memory work
  secretary

helper
  deaf
  blind
  narcotic addicts
  alcoholics
  mentally ill
  migrant workers
  remedial reading
  nursing
  underprivileged
  mentally retarded

library bookbinding

radio booth
  sound engineer

drama—acting

## Serving

officers
  financial secretary
  treasurer

librarian

greeter

building committee

nursery coordinator

young people
  Pioneer Girls
  King's Sons
  Christian Service
    Brigade
  Boy Scouts
  Girl Scouts

women's missionary
  circles

men's fellowship

music
  song leader
  soloist
  instrumentalist

nurse

kitchen help

handyman

carpenter

church drama productions

financial

accounting

audiovisual
  video-taping
  projectionist
  television
  photographer

helper
  narcotic addicts
  alcoholics
  migrant workers
  nursing
  underprivileged

music
  chancel choir director
  youth choir director
  children's choir director
  song leader
  choir member
  soloist
  trio
  duet
  quartet
  pianist—accompanist
      —soloist
  organist
  instrumentalist
  orchestra leader

music committee

office help
type
telephone

hospitality
meals
lodging

## Administration

boards and commissions
deacon
trustee
deaconess
Christian education
missionary
school
property
finance
membership
evangelistic
church services
social
building
planning

officers
financial secretary
treasurer
head usher

nursery coordinator

young people
youth sponsor
youth committee
single adults sponsor
Pioneer Girls
King's Sons
Christian Service
Brigade

women's missionary circle
leader

men's fellowship leader

Sunday school
assistant superintendent
department
coordinator—all
ages
class officer
class committees

librarian
cataloging

international student
ministry

camp
director
assistant director
administrative staff

radio booth operator

audiovisual room
coordinator

drama directing

coffeehouse ministry

vacation Bible school
director
committee
assistant

teen week director

## Ruling

boards and commissions
 school board
 deacon
 trustee
 property
 finance
 building
 planning

church services
 greeter
 head usher

church moderator
 vice moderator

vacation Bible school
 director

teen week director

Sunday school
 superintendent
 department coordinator

men's fellowship leader

women's fellowship leader

women's missionary circle
 leader

camp director

class officers

## Mercy

boards and commissions
 deacon
 deaconess

church services
 usher
 greeter

cassette ministry to
 shut-ins

hospitality
 meals
 lodging

visitation
 sick
 dying
 shut-ins
 hospitals
 rest homes
 telephone
 newcomers
 bereaved

missions
 committee
 missionary circles
 local gospel mission
 White Cross
 correspondent with
 missionaries
 furlough assistant

helper
 alcoholics
 mentally ill
 remedial reading
 nursing
 blind
 deaf
 gangs
 hungry and
 underprivileged
 mentally retarded
 migrant workers
 narcotic addict
 released prison
 offenders

*Giving*

| | |
|---|---|
| boards and commissions<br>    trustee<br>    missionary commission<br>    fund raising commission<br>    building commission<br>    school commission<br>    planning and<br>        development<br>    commission | food and money to help<br>    poor<br><br>hospitality<br>    meals<br>    lodging<br><br>sponsor and underwrite<br>    special missionary projects |

FITTING INTO A PLACE OF SERVICE. Now that you have checked areas of service you are willing to try, it is time to make an appointment with your pastor, minister of Christian education, or other church worker who can assist you in finding a specific place to serve in your church.

If you have never served before, or have not served in the areas that are currently open, be sure to ask the church worker for training. Don't try to be so brave as to work without help until you have some training and experience.

After you have mutually agreed upon an area of service, and have arranged for proper training and supervision, fill out the "My Commitment" form that follows this page. Be prepared to really commit yourself to doing an excellent job. Excellence breeds confidence if you are serving in the area for which you are gifted. Without the commitment, you may miss the opportunity to affirm your gift, because you would not have worked hard enough to have a good experience. Determining your gift will take work, but will lead to many years of effective, satisfying, and fruitful service once you find it.

Upon completion of your commitment form, you will soon begin to be trained and to serve. After three months of experience, you will want to evaluate your progress on the "Gift Evaluation" form following the "commitment" form. In addition, your supervisor, or the one who is working the closest with you, will evaluate you on the "Supervisor Evaluation" form included in this chapter. This time of evaluation will be very helpful to you in determining whether or not you should continue to test the gift in the area of service to which you have committed yourself.

If it is mutually agreed that you should pursue another gift or area of service, contact your church worker in charge of placement, and repeat the process, beginning with paragraph one of this chapter. This process should be continued until you find a satisfying, challenging, and fruitful place of service in keeping with your spiritual gift. Having diligently studied and prayed as you worked through this manual, you will find that your gift will become evident before too long, if not in your first area of service.

MY COMMITMENT. After reviewing the various areas of service corresponding to the spiritual gifts, I am willing to serve the Lord in the following way as soon as a position can be obtained:

_____

_____

This service will help me determine if I have the spiritual gift of _____

I will be trained and supervised in the following manner:

_____

_____

_____

I will be responsible for evaluating my progress (using the other forms provided) with one of the pastors or other spiritual leaders in the church. I will turn in these forms to the pastor by _____.
                        (date)

                Signed _____
                Date _____


GIFT EVALUATION FORM. Date of evaluation _____
Area of service completed _____
Spiritual gift tested _____
Describe the aspects of the work which you enjoyed most.

_____

Describe the aspects of the work which you didn't enjoy. __

_____

_____

What fruit did you see in your own life through your service?_____

_____

What fruit did you see in the lives of those you served? ____

_____

Do you believe that more learning and experience could possibly confirm the existence of this gift in you? _____

_____

Signed _____
Date _____


SUPERVISOR EVALUATION FORM. Name of worker ____

_____

Date of evaluation _____
Area of service completed _____
Spiritual gift tested _____

Evaluate the above-named worker in the following areas.
  1. Degree of spiritual motivation to do the task: _____

_____

  2. Degree of responsibility to the task: _____

_____

  3. Response of persons being served: _____

_____

  4. Do you believe he or she may have the above-mentioned spiritual gift? Explain. _____

_____

_____

Signed _____
Date _____

# APPENDIXES

Appendix I
Planning a spiritual gifts seminar

II
Structuring a spiritual gifts seminar

III
Illustrated score sheet for evaluations
one and two

IV
Guide to interpreting the results of
evaluation one

V
Guide to interpreting the results of
evaluation two

# APPENDIX I
## Planning a
## Spiritual Gifts Seminar

*Leader preparation*

This manual has been designed to give you an adequate background of information necessary to hold a spiritual gifts seminar. A thorough understanding of the biblical material and the evaluations is necessary. You should be able to clearly distinguish between the spiritual gifts after studying the sections called "Understanding the gifts" and "Evaluating yourself against each gift." The evaluation instructions and scoring can be mastered by doing the evaluations on yourself.

The following sections in this appendix will outline various concerns which you should take note of in overall planning.

*Advance notice of the seminar*

Promotion of the seminar should begin two months before the first session. The kind of publicity needed will depend on how much the people know about the subject of spiritual gifts. Some will be ready to sign up immediately after hearing of its nature and purpose. Others may be either unfamiliar with or confused by the subject and, therefore, not naturally responsive to general publicity. Both of these groups must become vitally interested through initial advertising.

Well-worded, descriptive announcements made during regular church services and in special bulletin inserts will build interest. These communications should contain stimulating appeals as to why every Christian should know and be using his spiritual gift. A key verse like 1 Peter 4:10, which shows that every Christian has a gift that he or she is to use, will help motivate them biblically. Testimonies from church members who are using their gifts will add a personal touch.

Three Sundays prior to the beginning of the seminar, all people (high school and above) who want to be involved should sign up. A posted list or bulletin insert with a registration section can be used. The time, place, cost, and duration of the course should be clearly shown. Posters and other spot reminders to register are helpful, also.

*Encouraging those who are already serving*

In every church there are faithful people who are serving Christ diligently. They may feel reasonably happy and fulfilled in their tasks. These people will be tempted to conclude that they do not need a seminar which stresses service. However, if they are not sure what their gifts are, they will lack a full, biblically based assurance that they are serving exactly where Christ would have them. When such people realize they have specific spiritual gifts to enable them to serve with power, their confidence and their effectiveness is greatly increased.

There are other benefits, too, for active Christians who know their spiritual gifts. First, they are saved from serving unsatisfyingly in positions that require spiritual gifts they do not possess. Too, they are rescued from taking on tasks inconsistent with the proper exercise of their gift.

Every participant in the church who does not know for certain what his gift is should take the seminar. For the uninvolved, it will provide the first step toward serving, and for those who are already serving, it will lead to maximum fruitfulness and confidence.

*The need for giving personal help*

Some people will not be able to grasp the material in the manual and work through it successfully on their own. Others may become confused at one point or another in the study, and feel incapable of completing it. Therefore, the leaders must always be available to give personal help when needed. Assisting someone to understand the biblical teaching on gifts, to evaluate himself or herself spiritually, and to find his or her peculiar area of service, is one of the most profitable uses of time. (See Ephesians 4:12-16.)

*Determining church needs*

Each gifted Christian is led to a local church to contribute to that spiritual body. Each individual is essential and must have a place to serve. No church is given an excess of gifted people who are not needed.

Since a spiritual gifts seminar brings to the surface gifted people, a list of current, challenging ministries must be prepared so each person can begin serving promptly. If the seminar is offered each year, an updated list of church needs, plus the gifts to be exercised in filling each need, should be available at all times.

The list of needs should include current tasks which need to be done to keep the present ministries fully staffed. In addition, a list of creative tasks which the church isn't carrying out should be available. These creative jobs stimulate vision in the church and provide vital opportunities for those who are willing to serve in a new ministry.

The pastor, Christian education director, and/or church ministry coordinators (Sunday school department heads, Sunday school superintendent, vacation Bible school coordinators, head usher, music director, etc.) should meet together for an orientation period prior to the beginning of the seminar. Each leader should draw up a list of service needs in his area by the fifth week of the seminar. When completed, the lists should be given to the pastor or other person conducting the seminar. The seminar leader must then decide which spiritual gifts might be exercised in meeting each need. See an example of this analysis below.

### Training those who have made commitments

The key to moving people from the seminar into effective service with their gifts is training. This might be done in a large group, a small group, or on an individual basis. The extent of need for training and the number of capable instructors in the church will determine what a church can do. Ultimately, the training will have to fit each church's situation. However, one thing is certain: the newly committed seminar graduates must be helped.

Example of church needs with suggested spiritual gifts:

CENTRAL BAPTIST CHURCH
PRESENT NEEDS ANALYZED BY SPIRITUAL GIFTS

| Area of need | Coordinator | Gifts used to meet needs |
|---|---|---|
| SUNDAY SCHOOL | | |
| beginner dept. | | |
| adult helper | dept. head | exhortation, serving, helps |

| Area of need | Coordinator | Gifts used to meet needs |
|---|---|---|
| primary dept. | | |
| record keeper | dept. head | helps, admin. |
| junior dept. | | |
| pianist | dept. head | helps, serving |
| young single | | |
| adult teacher | S. S. supt. | teaching, exhortation knowledge |

### WEDNESDAY NIGHT

| | | |
|---|---|---|
| Christian Service Brigade committee member | boy's work chairman | serving, admin., wisdom, discernment of spirits |

### MUSIC

| | | |
|---|---|---|
| children's choir director | music dir. | admin., helps, serving |
| soloist | music dir. | exhortation, helps, serving |

### OUTREACH

| | | |
|---|---|---|
| evangelistic calling | outreach director | wisdom, mercy, exhortation |
| home Bible study leader | H.B.S. leader | teaching, wisdom |
| gospel teams | outreach director | preaching, exhortation, faith |

### COMMITTEE MEMBERS

| | | |
|---|---|---|
| missionary | nominating committee | faith, admin., mercy, giving |
| property | nominating committee | wisdom, admin., helps, giving |

# APPENDIX II
## Structuring a Spiritual Gifts Seminar

There is no single, inflexible way of taking a group of Christians through the study on spiritual gifts. The studies can be broken down into a number of parts and taken one at a time. The manual lends itself very well to a one-quarter Sunday school class. This usually leaves three or four weeks at the end for further exploring any particularly important aspect of the study, or for studying material on the miraculous spiritual gifts and office gifts which this manual does not cover.

The illustration presented below explains one way of developing the seminar. It demonstrates how to coordinate the materials and the students' efforts.

Each session is scheduled for one hour. Obviously, the amount of time will depend on the size and makeup of the group. The tasks to be completed for each week are included under that week's responsibilities.

*First Week Session*

LEADER'S RESPONSIBILITIES

1. Have a registration sheet ready to circulate which requests name, address, and phone number of the student.
2. Type an attendance sheet in alphabetical order and provide boxes for checking attendance each week.
3. Present a general introduction and survey of the manual's content. Emphasize the importance of the study to your own church or group.

STUDENT'S RESPONSIBILITIES

1. Purchase the manual and attend the session.
2. Commit yourself to faithfully following through each week by completing the assigned study.
3. Pray that God will give you spiritual wisdom and insight regarding your gift so that you might maximize your service for him.

LEADER'S RESPONSIBILITIES

4. Ask for any questions concerning the course as a whole.
5. Assign the study in chapter one through the section on "Spiritual gifts."
6. Lead the group into the material in chapter one as time allows, helping them fill in some answers.

*Second Week Session*

1. Discuss the material assigned in chapter one, item by item. Have the students look up selected passages, but not all. Call on people from the roll so they won't come to class unprepared, thinking they can look up the answer at the time they are questioned.
2. Have each student tear out four copies of the assessment form two on page 52. These forms are to be filled in by the four available people who know the person best. Explain clearly how to complete the form. Tell the students they have six weeks to give out the forms, get them back, and compile the results. As the forms are returned, they should be scored.

1. Be prepared to discuss chapter one as assigned at the last session.

| LEADER'S RESPONSIBILITIES | STUDENT'S RESPONSIBILITIES |
|---|---|
| 3. Assign the study in chapter two on the first seven gifts. | |

*Third Week Session*

| | |
|---|---|
| 1. Discuss the material assigned in chapter two on the first seven gifts. | 1. Be prepared to discuss the study on the first seven spiritual gifts. |
| 2. Assign the study in chapter two on the last six gifts. | 2. Select the four people to whom you will give the evaluation forms, and give or mail them along with an explanation of instructions. |

*Fourth Week Session*

| | |
|---|---|
| 1. Discuss the material assigned in chapter two on the last six spiritual gifts. | 1. Be prepared to discuss the study on the last six gifts. |
| 2. Assign the study of chapters three and four. | |

*Fifth Week Session*

| | |
|---|---|
| 1. Discuss the material assigned in chapters three and four. | 1. Be prepared to discuss the study on chapters three and four. |
| 2. Assign the study of chapter five through "Personal preparation before using the gifts." | |

*Sixth Week Session*

| | |
|---|---|
| 1. Discuss the material assigned in chapter five. | 1. Be prepared to discuss the material in chapter five that was assigned. |
| 2. Assign the study of the remainder of chapter five. | 2. If you haven't received your evaluations back from others, contact them. |

*Seventh Week Session*

| | |
|---|---|
| 1. Discuss the material assigned in the | 1. Be prepared to discuss the material for the |

LEADER'S RESPONSIBILITIES    STUDENT'S RESPONSIBILITIES

remainder of chapter five.

2. Assign the material in chapters six and eight.

*Eighth Week Session*

1. Discuss the evaluations.
   a. Resolve any questions students have in understanding the questionnaire.
   b. Show the students how to score the evaluations and have them complete the scoring in class.
   c. Explain how to fill in the summary on page 77, 78 and have them complete it in class.
2. Assign the study of chapters nine and ten.
3. Hand out a complete list of the present needs in your church (see sample copy on page 100). Encourage the students to make some tentative choices after completing the evaluation of each gift in chapter nine and checking the areas of interest in chapter ten.
4. Encourage the students to pray that God will direct them to the place where they should begin serving.

*Ninth Week Session*

1. Resolve any questions

remainder of chapter five.

1. Have the evaluation forms completed and be ready to score them.

1. Have the following

105

| LEADER'S RESPONSIBILITIES | STUDENT'S RESPONSIBILITIES |
|---|---|
| the students have in understanding the evaluation of themselves against each gift. | complete: |
| 2. Have the ministry coordinators ready to talk with the students about service. | a. the evaluation of yourself against each gift. |
| 3. Explain the forms on pages 95, 96. | b. the selection of areas of service as given in chapter ten that are consistent with your top four gift possibilities. |
| 4. Indicate to the group that you will be conducting a group evaluation session in about three months to assess overall progress of seminar participants. | c. the tentative selection of areas of service in your church which require your possible gifts. |
| | 2. Be prepared to sign a "My Commitment" form after consulting with one or more ministry coordinators who will be in attendance at the last session. |

# APPENDIX III
## Illustrated Score Sheet for Evaluations One and Two

*PERSONAL (AND OTHERS') ASSESSMENT*
*OF MY PREFERENCES AND TENDENCIES*

1. I prefer situations in my church where I am:
   - ⓐ a speaker
   - b. in a discussion group
   - c. just a listener
2. If asked to speak, I prefer speaking to:
   - ⓐ large groups
   - ⓑ small groups
   - c. individuals

*Score Sheet*

| PREACHING | TEACHING | KNOWLEDGE | WISDOM | EXHORTATION | FAITH | DISCERNMENT OF SPIRITS | HELPS | SERVING | ADMINISTRATION | RULING | MERCY | GIVING | |
|---|---|---|---|---|---|---|---|---|---|---|---|---|---|
| (X) | (X) | | | | | | | | | (X) | | | (1a) |
| | X | X | X | X | X | X | | | X | | | | 1b |
| | | | | | | | | | | | X | | 1c |
| (X) | (X) | | | (X) | | | | | | | | | (2a) |
| | (X) | (X) | (X) | | (X) | (X) | | | (X) | | | | (2b) |
| | | | | | | | X | | | | X | | 2c |
| | | | | | | X | | | | | | | 25h |

| | PREACHING | TEACHING | KNOWLEDGE | WISDOM | EXHORTATION | FAITH | DISCERNMENT OF SPIRITS | HELPS | SERVING | ADMINISTRATION | RULING | MERCY | GIVING |
|---|---|---|---|---|---|---|---|---|---|---|---|---|---|
| TOTAL CIRCLED | 2 | 3 | 1 | 1 | 1 | 1 | 1 | — | — | 1 | 1 | — | — |
| % CIRCLED | 13 | 19 | 6 | 6 | 6 | 6 | 6 | — | — | 6 | 6 | — | — |

107

# APPENDIX IV
## Guide to Interpreting
## the Results of Evaluation One

After you finish Evaluation One, you may find that you have not yet been able to gain clear direction regarding your gift. The percentage of circled responses may be very similar for three or four gifts. You must now analyze the responses so as to determine your predominant preferences and tendencies.

In the multiple choice setting, you may have selected preferences that were true, given the options. However, if your selected preferences had been compared with one another, probably one of them would have been stronger than the others.

The following analysis describes each gift in terms of the preferences and tendencies of one with that gift. To use this analysis form, proceed in the following manner:

1. Note the names of the gifts for which you had the similar preference percentages.

   a._____
   b._____
   c._____
   d._____
   e._____

2. Take the score sheet and locate the column with the name of the gift noted in 1a above. Proceed down the column in search of the circled X's. Whenever you find a circled X, move across the score sheet from the X to the far left-hand column, where the numbered responses are given (2c, 3b, etc.).

3. After locating the numbered response corresponding to the circled X, proceed to the analysis of that gift below. Find the numbered response under the gift analysis which corresponds to the numbered response for the circled X in the score sheet. Circle that numbered response in the analysis.

4. Go back to the score sheet, find the second circled X and the corresponding numbered response, and circle that response under the same gift analysis below.

5. Repeat this procedure until all of the circled X's on the score sheet are also circled under the gift analysis below.

6. Repeat the procedure in 2 above for each of the gifts noted in 1.
7. Then analyze the results by the following inquiry:
   a. Compare the circled responses of all the gifts analyzed in 2 above, noting when a particular preference or tendency has been circled under more than one gift. For example, if preaching and teaching were two of the gifts being analyzed, under the analysis both would have circled preference 1a—"I prefer situations in which I am a speaker." Since there are a number of gifts which have the same preferences and tendencies, these should be noted.

   | Gifts with the same preferences | Preferences used twice or more |
   |---|---|
   | 1)_____ | _____ |
   | 2)_____ | _____ |
   | 3)_____ | _____ |
   | 4)_____ | _____ |
   | 5)_____ | _____ |
   | 6)_____ | _____ |
   | 7)_____ | _____ |

   b. Think over the remaining preferences which have not been circled twice, and try to discern if there seem to be three or four responses which are not exactly the same preference but could be considered similar. Summarize the similar preferences and tendencies below.

   | Gifts with similar preferences | Summary |
   |---|---|
   | 1)_____ | _____ |
   | 2)_____ | _____ |
   | 3)_____ | _____ |

   c. Taking the results in a and b above, decide which of the gifts in 1 above is most like these same and similar preferences. The decision may be difficult, but always remember that the evaluation is to be used only as a guide for purposes of channeling you into service. The ultimate determination of your gift will take place through service itself.
   d. The same and similar preferences and tendencies, along with overall analysis, seem to indicate that my gift might be_____

GIFT ANALYSIS
IN TERMS OF PREFERENCES AND TENDENCIES

### I. Gift of Prophecy (Preaching)

1a I prefer situations in my church in which I am a speaker.

2a I prefer speaking to large groups.

3b When faced with counseling another person about his problems, I tend to give him the best biblical solution I can think of even if I'm not totally confident about my counsel.

4a When I begin to prepare for a talk to other Christians, I am normally motivated to emphasize the truths of basic Bible themes, so as to lead the listener to a clear-cut decision in the meeting.

6c When I approach my personal devotions, I most prefer to relate to the verses emotionally, so as to get a personal blessing.

7b If I have my choice of passages to study, I mostly choose ones which are very practical.

7d If I have my choice of passages to study, I mostly choose ones which have great emotional appeal to my Christian life.

8b When I give a testimony, I tend to indicate some area of doctrine that has come alive to me through an experience and/or verse I've shared.

8c When I give a testimony, I tend to emphasize the practical application of some verse(s) to my life.

11a When evaluating another Christian's spiritual condition, I tend to point out errors in his understanding of the Christian life.

13a In an organization, I prefer to lead a group.

20d If given a choice regarding involvement in a Sunday school class lesson, I tend to favor presenting the lesson with the content, illustrations, and applications available.

21a With regard to decisions made from my speaking, I prefer to see an immediate commitment at the meeting by individuals in the group.

23d When called upon to serve, I am most naturally

motivated to help in situations in which there are specific spiritual needs (for commitment, faith, dealing with sin, etc.).

24a When speaking before people, I sense an inner urgency to persuade people to make spiritual decisions and commitments right then.

24b When speaking before people I find it easy to accept the authority of the Scriptures without hesitation.

## II. *Gift of Teaching*

1a I prefer situations in my church in which I am a speaker.

1b I prefer situations in my church in which I am in a discussion group.

2a I prefer speaking to large groups.

2b I prefer speaking to small groups.

3b When faced with counseling another person about his problems, I tend to give him the best biblical solution I can think of, even if I'm not totally confident about my counsel.

4b When I begin to prepare for a talk to other Christians, I am normally motivated to carefully organize a biblical passage in a systematic way, so that the listener clearly understands it.

5b When listening to others speak, I dislike talks which heavily emphasize illustrations and applications without logical order and doctrine.

6a When I approach my personal devotions, I most prefer to search out how the verses I'm studying add to my understanding of doctrine.

7a If I have my choice of passages to study, I mostly choose ones which are rich in doctrine.

7c If I have my choice of passages to study, I mostly choose ones which are controversial or difficult to understand.

8b When I give a testimony, I tend to indicate some area of doctrine that has come alive to me through an experience and/or verses I've shared.

11a When evaluating another Christian's spiritual condition, I tend to point out errors in his understanding of the Christian life.

20b If given a choice regarding involvement in a

Sunday school class lesson, I tend to favor organizing available content and illustrations for presentation of the truths.

21c With regard to decisions made from my speaking, I prefer to have an opportunity to explore the decision in depth through discussion.

23b When called upon to serve, I am most naturally motivated to help in situations in which there are specific mental needs (lack of understanding of Scripture, need to find God's will in a certain area, etc.).

24c When speaking before people, I am inwardly compelled to prepare well and speak carefully.

### III. Gift of Knowledge

1b I prefer situations in my church in which I am in a discussion group.

2b I prefer speaking to small groups.

3c When faced with counseling another person about his problems, I tend to prefer sharing biblical insights, avoiding discussions about feelings.

4c When I begin to prepare for a talk to other Christians, I am normally motivated to instruct on doctrinal topics, to enable the listener to have a better understanding of these subject areas.

5b When listening to others speak, I tend to dislike talks which heavily emphasize illustrations and applications without logical order and doctrine.

6a When I approach my personal devotions, I most prefer to search out how the verses I'm studying add to my understanding of doctrine.

7a If I have my choice of passages to study, I mostly choose ones which are rich in doctrine.

7c If I have my choice of passages to study, I mostly choose ones which are controversial or difficult to understand.

8b When I give a testimony, I tend to indicate some area of doctrine that has come alive to me through an experience and/or verses I've shared.

11a When evaluating another Christian's spiritual condition, I tend to point out errors in his understanding of the Christian life.

17a My reaction to the needs of others tends to be slow because I don't know what to do.

20a If given a choice regarding involvement in a Sunday school class lesson, I would tend to favor doing the biblical research and study to provide the lesson content.

21c With regard to decisions made from my speaking, I prefer to have an opportunity to explore the decision in depth through discussion.

23b When called upon to serve, I am most naturally motivated to help in situations in which there are specific mental needs (lack of understanding Scripture, need to find God's will in a certain area, etc.).

24d When speaking before people, I have a tendency to encourage thought-life changes and decisions more than conduct changes.

24e When speaking before people, I feel most comfortable presenting a thorough, detailed study of a biblical passage or topic.

IV. *Gift of Wisdom*

1b I prefer situations in my church in which I am in a discussion group.

2b I prefer speaking to small groups.

2c I prefer speaking to individuals.

3d When faced with counseling another person about his problems, I tend to urge him to follow my counsel, because I honestly believe God often helps me to see solutions to others' problems.

4d When I begin to prepare for a talk to Christians, I am normally motivated to stress application of passages that emphasize practical truths so that the listener's conduct can be refined.

5a When listening to others speak, I tend to dislike in-depth doctrinal studies without applications.

6b When I approach my personal devotions, I most prefer to analyze the verses with the purpose of changing specific areas of my conduct.

7b If I have my choice of passages to study, I mostly choose ones which are very practical.

8c When I give a testimony, I tend to emphasize the practical application of some verse(s) to my life.

16d If a group is meeting and no assigned leader is
there, I would tend to call someone to find out
who the real leader is.

17c My reaction to the needs of others tends to be
deliberate, because I want to make sure I've
thought it through thoroughly.

20c If given a choice regarding involvement in a
Sunday school class lesson, I would tend to favor
thinking up original applications for the lesson,
given the organized content.

21b With regard to decisions made from my
speaking, I prefer to do follow-up counseling
directed at long-range changes in conduct.

22b If I were a leader faced with two Christians in
the church who couldn't get along, I would tend
to talk to them about changing their attitudes.

23b When called upon to serve, I am most naturally
motivated to help in situations in which there
are specific mental needs (lack of understanding
of Scripture, need to find God's will in a certain
area, etc.)

24f When speaking before people, I have a tendency
to give biblical insights on continually knowing
and doing God's will.

## V. *Gift of Exhortation*

1b I prefer situations in my church in which I am
in a discussion group.

2a I prefer speaking to large groups.

3a When faced with counseling another person
about his problems, I tend to identify deeply
with his situation.

3d When faced with counseling another person
about his problems, I tend to urge him to follow
my counsel, because I honestly believe God often
helps me see solutions to others' problems.

4e When I begin to prepare for a talk to other
Christians, I am normally motivated to take one
verse and outline practical, specific steps of
action for the listener to follow.

5a When listening to others speak, I tend to dislike
in-depth doctrinal studies without applications.

6b When I approach my personal devotions, I most

prefer to analyze the verses with the purpose of changing specific areas of conduct.

7b If I have my choice of passages to study, I mostly choose ones which are very practical.

8a When I give a testimony, I tend to encourage or console others rather than just share a verse or experience.

10b When conversing with other Christians, I tend to exhort them to embrace certain goals and actions.

11b When evaluating another Christian's spiritual condition, I tend to sense areas of right and wrong conduct in his life and point out some solutions.

17b My reaction to the needs of others tends to be quick because I usually sense what needs to be done.

21b With regard to decisions made from my speaking, I prefer to do follow-up counseling directed at long-range changes in conduct.

22b If I were a leader faced with two Christians in the church who couldn't get along, I would tend to talk to them about changing their attitudes.

23c When called upon to serve, I am most naturally motivated to help in situations in which there are specific emotional needs (fear, anxiety, frustration, moods due to pain or trials, etc.).

24g When speaking before people, I have a tendency to feel real concern for those in difficulty, and to suggest ways to help them.

## VI. *Gift of Faith*

1b I prefer situations in my church in which I am in a discussion group.

2b I prefer speaking to small groups.

3b When faced with counseling another person about his problems, I tend to give him the best biblical solution I can think of, even if I'm not totally confident about my counsel.

6c When I approach my personal devotions, I most prefer to relate to the verses emotionally, so as to get a personal blessing.

7b If I have my choice of passages to study, I mostly choose ones which are very practical.

8a When I give a testimony, I tend to encourage or console others rather than just share a verse or experience.

9a With regard to planning for the future of my church, I tend to have confidence about what the church should do.

9c With regard to planning for the future of my church, I tend to be more concerned with envisioning end results than with the details involved in getting there.

9d With regard to planning for the future of my church, I tend to have a great desire to see quick growth in the church's ministries.

10b When conversing with other Christians, I tend to exhort them to embrace certain goals and actions.

15a If asked to lead in a church program somewhere, I would tend to choose a position which involved comprehensive planning for the future.

17b My reaction to the needs of others tends to be quick because I usually sense what needs to be done.

19e With regard to financial matters, I tend to see money as a means for carrying out ministries and meeting needs, more than for construction of buildings, payment of salaries, etc.

21a With regard to decisions made from my speaking, I prefer to see an immediate commitment at the meeting by individuals in the group.

23d When called upon to serve, I am most naturally motivated to help in situations in which there are specific spiritual needs (for commitment, faith, dealing with sin, etc.).

25a Generally speaking, I have a tendency to visualize future goals, and to work toward them in spite of difficulties.

VII. *Gift of Discernment of Spirits*

1b I prefer situations in my church where I am in a discussion group.

2b I prefer speaking to small groups.

3d When faced with counseling another person about his problems, I tend to urge him to follow my counsel, because I honestly believe God often helps me see solutions to others' problems.

6b When I approach my personal devotions, I most prefer to analyze the verses with the purpose of changing specific areas of my conduct.

7c If I have my choice of passages to study, I mostly choose ones which are controversial or difficult to understand.

8c When I give a testimony, I tend to emphasize the practical application of some verses to my life.

10a When conversing with other Christians, I tend to probe them to determine their true spiritual condition and needs.

11b When evaluating another Christian's spiritual condition, I tend to sense areas of right and wrong conduct in his life, and to point out some solutions.

15d If asked to lead in a church program somewhere, I would tend to choose a position which involved evaluating personnel for various leadership positions.

17c My reaction to the needs of others tends to be deliberate, because I want to make sure I've thought it through thoroughly.

18a In regard to decision making, I tend to make decisions easily and with confidence.

21c With regard to decisions made from my speaking, I prefer to have an opportunity to explore the decision in depth through discussion.

23d When called upon to serve, I am most naturally motivated to help in situations in which there are specific spiritual needs (for commitment, faith, dealing with sin, etc.).

25b Generally speaking, I have a tendency to be wise in discerning the character quality of another person.

25c Generally speaking, I have a tendency to accurately detect weaknesses and pitfalls when evaluating opportunities and situations.

25h Generally speaking, I have a tendency to see through others' actions to their real motives and inner attitudes.

VIII. *Gift of Helps*

2c I prefer speaking to individuals.

3a When faced with counseling another person about his problems, I tend to identify deeply with his situation.

5a When listening to others speak, I tend to be strongly impressed with exhortations to serve other Christians.

6c When I approach my personal devotions, I most prefer to relate to the verses emotionally, so as to get a personal blessing.

7b If I have my choice of passages to study, I mostly choose ones which are very practical.

8c When I give a testimony, I tend to emphasize the practical application of some verse(s) to my life.

12b When presented with a physical or spiritual need, I tend to respond best if someone calls and asks me to help fill it.

12c When presented with a physical or spiritual need, I tend to not respond if the need requires considerable personal preparation.

12d When presented with a physical or spiritual need, I tend to not respond if the need involves a lot of organizational detail and red tape.

13b In an organization, I prefer to be a follower under another's leadership.

14c When given a task which needs to be done now, I prefer to be told by a competent leader exactly what to do.

14e When given a task to do, I tend to favor doing it myself rather than delegating it.

16b If a group is meeting and no assigned leader is there, I would tend to let the meeting proceed with no direct leadership.

18c In regard to decision making when the facts are clear, I tend to rely on others whom I believe are more capable of sorting out the issues in the decision.

23a When called upon to serve, I am most naturally
   motivated to help in situations in which there
   are specific material needs (food, buildings,
   equipment, money).

## IX. *Gift of Serving*

2c I prefer speaking to individuals.

3a When faced with counseling another person
   about his problems, I tend to identify deeply
   with his situation.

5a When listening to others speak, I tend to dislike
   in-depth doctrinal studies without applications.

5c When listening to others speak, I tend to be
   strongly impressed with exhortations to serve
   other Christians.

6c When I approach my personal devotions, I most
   prefer to relate to the verses emotionally, so as
   to get a personal blessing.

7b If I have my choice of passages to study, I
   mostly choose ones which are very practical.

8c When I give a testimony, I tend to emphasize
   the practical application of some verse(s) to my
   life.

12a When presented with a physical or spiritual
   need, I tend to respond on my own initiative to
   try to meet it if I can.

12d When presented with a physical or spiritual
   need, I tend to not respond if the need involves a
   lot of organizational detail.

13a In an organization, I prefer to lead a group.

14b When given a task which needs to be done now,
   I tend to leave it for another task if the second
   one seems more important at the time.

14d When given a task which needs to be done now,
   I tend to be concerned with doing a high quality
   and thorough job.

14e When given a task to do, I tend to favor doing it
   myself rather than delegating it.

16a If a group is meeting and no assigned leader is
   there, I would tend to assume the leadership.

17b My reaction to the needs of others tends to be
   quick because I usually sense what needs to be
   done.

23a When called upon to serve, I am most naturally
motivated to help in situations in which there
are specific material needs (food, buildings,
equipment, money).

25d Generally speaking, I have a tendency to have
great energy and stamina for working on and
meeting the practical needs of others.

## X. *Gift of Administration*

1b I prefer situations in my church in which I am
in a discussion group.

2b I prefer speaking to small groups.

9b With regard to planning for the future of my
church, I tend to be concerned about and willing
to do detailed, deliberate work on the plans.

11c When evaluating another Christian's spiritual
condition, I tend to be critical of areas of his life
which are not disciplined and well ordered.

13a In an organization, I prefer to lead a group.

14a When given a task which needs to be done now,
I tend to complete it before taking on another
task.

14d When given a task which needs to be done now,
I tend to be concerned with doing a high quality
and thorough job.

15c If asked to lead in a church program somewhere,
I would tend to choose a position which involved
harmonizing various viewpoints for a decision.

15b If asked to lead in a church program somewhere,
I would tend to choose a position which involved
detailed planning and decision making for the
present.

15e If asked to lead in a church program somewhere,
I would tend to choose a position which involved
drawing up procedures and guidelines for
effective inner working of the church.

16c If a group is meeting and no assigned leader is
there, I would tend to appoint or ask someone in
the group to lead.

17c My reaction to the needs of others tends to be
deliberate because I want to make sure I've
thought it through thoroughly.

18a In regard to decision making, I tend to make decisions easily and with confidence.

19d With regard to financial matters, I tend to feel deeply that such matters should be handled in an orderly and prudent manner.

22a If I were a leader faced with two Christians in the church who couldn't get along, I would tend to change one person's responsibilities and position at the point of conflict.

23a When called upon to serve, I am most naturally motivated to help in situations in which there are specific material needs (food, buildings, equipment, money).

## XI. *Gift of Ruling*

1b I prefer situations in my church in which I am in a discussion group.

3b When faced with counseling another person about his problems, I tend to give him the best biblical solution I can think of, even if I'm not totally confident about my counsel.

5b When listening to others speak, I tend to dislike talks which heavily emphasize illustrations and applications without logical order and doctrine.

11c When evaluating another Christian's spiritual condition, I tend to be critical of areas of his/her life which are not disciplined and well ordered.

13a In an organization, I prefer to lead a group.

14a When given a task which needs to be done now, I tend to complete it before taking on another task.

14d When given a task which needs to be done now, I tend to be concerned with doing a high quality and thorough job.

15c If asked to lead in a church program somewhere, I would tend to choose a position which involved harmonizing various viewpoints for a decision.

15f If asked to lead in a church program somewhere, I would tend to choose a position which involved delegating responsibilities to others.

16a If a group is meeting and no assigned leader is there, I would tend to assume the leadership.

17c My reaction to the needs of others tends to be

deliberate because I want to make sure I've
thought it through thoroughly.

18a In regard to decision making, I tend to make
decisions easily and with confidence.

19d With regard to financial matters, I tend to feel
deeply that such matters should be handled in
an orderly and prudent manner.

22a If I were a leader faced with two Christians in
the church who couldn't get along, I would tend
to change one person's responsibilities and
position at the point of conflict.

23a When called upon to serve, I am most naturally
motivated to help in situations in which there
are material needs (food, buildings, equipment,
money, etc.).

25e Generally speaking, I have a tendency to be
sensitive to overall organizational direction more
than minority, individual opinions.

## XII. *Gift of Mercy*

1c I prefer situations in my church in which I am
only a listener.

2c I prefer speaking to individuals.

3a When faced with counseling another person
about his problems, I tend to identify deeply
with his situation.

3b When faced with counseling another person
about his problems, I tend to give him the best
biblical solution I can think of, even if I'm not
totally confident about my counsel.

5c When listening to others speak, I tend to be
strongly impressed by exhortations to serve
other Christians.

6c When I approach my personal devotions, I
mostly prefer to relate to the verses emotionally
so as to get a personal blessing.

7b If I have my choice of passages to study, I
mostly choose ones which are very practical.

7d If I have my choice of passages to study, I
mostly choose ones which have great emotional
appeal to my Christian life.

8a When I give a testimony, I tend to encourage or

console others rather than just share a verse or experience.

13b In an organization, I prefer to be a follower under another's leadership.

14e When given a task to do, I tend to favor doing it myself rather than delegating it.

17b My reaction to the needs of others tends to be quick, because I usually sense what needs to be done.

18b In regard to decision making, I tend to lack firmness because of people's feelings.

22c If I were a leader faced with two Christians in the church who couldn't get along, I would tend to leave the situation alone for fear of offending them and making it worse.

23c When called upon to serve, I am most naturally motivated to help in situations in which there are specific emotional needs (fear, anxiety, frustration, moods due to pain or trials, etc.).

25f Generally speaking, I have a tendency to help meet obvious needs without measuring the worthiness of the recipient or evaluating his real needs.

## XIII. *Gift of Giving*

3a When faced with counseling another person about his problems, I tend to identify deeply with his situation.

5a When listening to others speak, I tend to dislike in-depth doctrinal studies without applications.

5c When listening to others speak, I tend to be strongly impressed with exhortations to serve other Christians.

6c When I approach my personal devotions, I most prefer to relate to the verses emotionally, so as to get a personal blessing.

7b If I have my choice of passages to study, I mostly choose ones which are very practical.

12a When presented with a physical or spiritual need, I tend to respond on my own initiative to try to meet it if I can.

12e When presented with a physical or spiritual problem, I tend to respond with money and possessions.

14e When given a task to do, I tend to favor doing it myself rather than delegating it.

17b My reaction to the needs of others tends to be quick because I usually sense what needs to be done.

19a With regard to financial matters, I tend to be able to make wise investments and gain wealth.

19b With regard to financial matters, I tend to be moved to give all I can to people and organizations I consider worthy.

19c With regard to financial matters, I tend to want assurances that the money I give will be used wisely.

19d With regard to financial matters, I tend to feel deeply that such matters should be handled in an orderly and prudent manner.

19f With regard to financial matters, I tend to work hard so I can meet legitimate needs.

23a When called upon to serve, I am most naturally motivated to help in situations in which there are specific material needs (food, buildings, equipment, etc.).

25g Generally speaking, I have a tendency to desire positive results and high quality in the things to which I give my efforts and money.

# APPENDIX V
## Guide to Interpreting
## the Results of Evaluation Two

After you finish Evaluation Two, you may find that you still have not been able to gain clear direction regarding your gift. The percentage of circled responses may be very similar for three or four gifts. You must now analyze the responses so as to determine your predominant preferences and tendencies.

In the multiple choice setting, you may have selected preferences that were true, given the options. However, if your selected preferences had been compared with one another, probably one of them would have been stronger than the others.

The following analysis describes each gift in terms of the preferences and tendencies of one who possesses that gift. To use this analysis form, proceed in the following manner:

1. Note the name of the gifts for which you had similar preference percentages.
   a._____
   b._____
   c._____
   d._____
   e._____
2. Take the score sheet and locate the column with the name of the gift noted in 1a above. Proceed down the column in search of the circled X's. Whenever you find a circled X, move across the score sheet from the X to the far left-hand column where the numbered responses are given (2c, 3b, etc.).
3. After locating the numbered response corresponding to the circled X, proceed to the analysis of that gift below. Find the numbered response under the gift analysis which corresponds to the numbered response for the circled X in the score sheet. Circle that numbered response in the analysis.
4. Go back to the score sheet, find the second circled X and the corresponding numbered response, and circle that response under the same gift analysis below.
5. Repeat this procedure until all of the circled X's on

the score sheet are also circled under the gift analysis below.

6. Repeat the procedure in 2 above for each of the gifts noted in 1.
7. Then analyze the results by the following inquiry:
    a. Compare the circled responses of all the gifts analyzed in 2 above, noting when a particular preference or tendency has been circled under more than one gift. For example, if preaching and teaching were two of the gifts being analyzed, under the analysis both would have circled preference 1a: "I prefer situations in which I am a speaker." Since a number of gifts have the same preferences and tendencies, these should be noted.

       | *Gifts with the same preferences* | *Preferences used twice or more* |
       |---|---|
       | 1)_____ | _____ |
       | 2)_____ | _____ |
       | 3)_____ | _____ |
       | 4)_____ | _____ |
       | 5)_____ | _____ |
       | 6)_____ | _____ |
       | 7)_____ | _____ |

    b. Think over the remaining preferences which have not been circled twice, and try to discern if there seem to be three or four responses which are not exactly the same preference but could be considered similar. Summarize the similar preferences and tendencies below.

       | *Gifts with similar preferences* | *Summary* |
       |---|---|
       | 1)_____ | _____ |
       | 2)_____ | _____ |
       | 3)_____ | _____ |

    c. Taking the results in a and b above, decide which of the gifts in 1 above is most like these same and similar preferences. The decision may be difficult, but always remember that the evaluation is to be used only as a guide for purposes of channeling you into service. The ultimate determination of your gift will take place through service.
    d. The same and similar preferences and tendencies along with overall analysis seem to indicate that

my gift might be_____

_____ .

## GIFT ANALYSIS
## IN TERMS OF PREFERENCES AND TENDENCIES

### I. *Gift of Prophecy (preaching)*

1a He/she prefers situations in the church in which he/she is a speaker.

2a If asked to speak, he/she prefers to speak to large groups.

3b When faced with counseling another person about problems, he/she tends to give the person the best biblical solution he/she can think of, even if not totally confident about the counsel.

4a When he/she begins to prepare for talks to other Christians, he/she is normally motivated to emphasize the truths of basic Bible themes so as to lead the listeners to a clear-cut decision in the meeting.

5b When giving a testimony, he/she tends to indicate some area of doctrine that has come alive through an experience or a shared verse.

5c When he/she gives a testimony, he tends to emphasize the practical application of some verses to his/her life.

8a If a person were to ask him/her to evaluate another's spiritual condition, he/she would tend to point out errors in that person's mental understanding of the Christian life.

10a In an organization, he/she prefers to lead a group.

17d When called upon to serve, he/she is most naturally motivated to help in situations in which there are specific spiritual needs (for commitment, faith, dealing with sin, etc.).

18a When speaking before people, he/she has a tendency to try to persuade people to make spiritual decisions and commitments right then.

### II. *Gift of Teaching*

1a He/she prefers situations in the church in which he/she is a speaker.

1b He/she prefers situations in the church in which he/she is in a discussion group.

2a If asked to speak, he/she prefers to speak to large groups.

2b If asked to speak, he/she prefers to speak to small groups.

3b When faced with counseling another person about problems, he/she tends to give the person the best biblical solution he/she can think of, even if not totally confident about the counsel.

4b When preparing for talks to other Christians, he/she is normally motivated to carefully organize a biblical passage in a systematic way so that the listeners clearly understand it.

5b When giving a testimony, he/she tends to indicate some area of doctrine that has come alive through an experience or a shared verse.

8a If a person were to ask him or her to evaluate another's spiritual condition, he/she would tend to point out errors in that person's mental understanding of the Christian life.

17b When called upon to serve, he/she is most naturally motivated to help in situations in which there are specific mental needs (lack of understanding of Scripture, need to find God's will in a certain area, etc.).

18b When speaking before people, he/she has a tendency to prepare well and speak carefully.

### III. Gift of Knowledge

1b He/she prefers situations in the church in which he/she is in a discussion group.

2b If asked to speak, he/she prefers to speak to small groups.

3c When faced with counseling another person about problems, he/she tends to prefer sharing biblical insights, and avoiding discussions about feelings.

4c When preparing for talks to other Christians, he/she is normally motivated to instruct on doctrinal topics, to enable the listeners to have a better understanding of these subjects.

5b When giving a testimony, he/she tends to

indicate some area of doctrine that has come alive through an experience or a shared verse.

8a If a person were to ask him/her to evaluate another's spiritual condition, he/she would tend to point out errors in that person's mental understanding of the Christian life.

14a His/her reaction to the needs of others tends to be slow, because of not knowing what to do.

17b When called upon to serve, he/she is most naturally motivated to help in situations in which there are specific mental needs (lack of understanding of Scripture, need to find God's will in a certain area, etc.).

18c When speaking before people, he/she has the tendency to encourage thought-life decisions more than conduct changes.

18d When speaking before people, he/she has a tendency to have little interest in emotional commitments unless they are based on clear biblical teaching.

## IV. *Gift of Wisdom*

1b He/she prefers situations in the church in which he/she is in a discussion group.

2b If asked to speak, he/she prefers to speak to small groups.

2c If asked to speak, he/she prefers to speak to individuals.

3d When faced with counseling another person about problems, he/she tends to urge the person to follow his/her counsel, because he/she honestly believes God helps him/her see the solutions to others' problems.

4d When preparing for talks to other Christians, he/she is normally motivated to stress application of passages that emphasize practical truths so that the listeners can refine their conduct.

5a When giving a testimony, he/she tends to encourage or console others rather than just share a verse or experience.

5c When giving a testimony, he/she tends to emphasize the practical application of some verses to his/her life.

13c If a group is meeting and no assigned leader is there, he/she would tend to call someone to find out who the real leader is.

14c His/her reaction to the needs of others tends to be deliberate, because of wanting to make sure he/she has thought it through thoroughly.

17b When called upon to serve, he/she is most naturally motivated to help in situations in which there are specific mental needs (lack of understanding of Scripture, need to find God's will in a certain area, etc.).

## V. Gift of Exhortation

1b He/she prefers situations in the church in which he/she is in a discussion group.

2a If asked to speak, he/she prefers to speak to large groups.

3a When faced with counseling another person about problems, he/she tends to identify deeply with the person's situation.

3d When faced with counseling another person about problems, he/she tends to urge the person to follow the counsel, because he/she honestly believes God helps him/her see the solutions to others' problems.

4e When he/she begins to prepare for talks to other Christians, he/she is normally motivated to take one verse and outline practical and specific steps of action for the listener to follow.

5a When giving a testimony, he/she tends to encourage or console others, rather than just share a verse or experience.

7b When conversing with other Christians, he/she tends to exhort them to embrace certain goals and actions.

8b If a person asks him/her to evaluate another's spiritual condition, he/she would tend to sense areas of right and wrong conduct in that person's life, and to point out some solutions.

14b His/her reaction to the needs of others tends to be quick, because he/she usually senses what needs to be done.

17c When called upon to serve, he/she is most

naturally motivated to help in situations in which there are specific emotional needs (fear, **anxiety,** frustration, moods due to pain and trials, etc.).

## VI. *Gift of Faith*

1b He/she prefers situations in the church in which he/she is in a discussion group.

2b If asked to speak, he/she prefers to speak to small groups.

3b When faced with counseling another person about problems, he/she tends to give the person the best biblical solution he/she can think of, even if not totally confident about the counsel.

6a With regard to planning for the future of his/her church, he/she tends to have positive confidence about what the church should do.

6b With regard to planning for the future of his/her church, he/she tends to be more concerned with envisioning end results than with the details involved in getting there.

6c With regard to planning for the future of his/her church, he/she tends to have a great desire to see quick growth in the ministries of the church.

7b When conversing with other Christians, he/she tends to exhort them to embrace certain goals and actions.

14b His/her reaction to the needs of others tends to be quick, because he/she senses what needs to be done most of the time.

16d With regard to financial matters, he/she tends to be moved to give all he can to people and organizations he/she considers worthy.

17d When called upon to serve, he/she is most naturally motivated to help in situations in which there are specific spiritual needs (for commitment, faith, dealing with sin, etc.).

## VII. *Gift of Discernment of Spirits*

1b He/she prefers situations in the church in which he/she is in a discussion group.

2b If asked to speak, he/she prefers to speak to small groups.

3d When faced with counseling another person

about problems, he/she tends to urge the person to follow his counsel, because he/she honestly believes God helps him/her see the solutions to others' problems.

5c When giving a testimony, he/she tends to emphasize the practical application of some verses to his/her life.

7a When conversing with other Christians, he/she tends to probe them to determine their true spiritual condition and needs.

8b If a person asks him/her to evaluate another's spiritual condition, he/she would tend to sense areas of right and wrong conduct in that person's life, and to point out some solutions.

12c If asked to lead somewhere in the church program, he/she would tend to choose a position which involved evaluating personnel for various leadership positions.

14c His/her reaction to the needs of others tends to be deliberate, because of wanting to make sure he/she has thought it through thoroughly.

17d When called upon to serve, he/she is most naturally motivated to help in situations in which there are specific spiritual needs (for commitment, faith, dealing with sin, etc.).

VIII. *Gift of Helps*

2c If asked to speak, he/she prefers to speak to individuals.

3a When faced with counseling another person about problems, he/she tends to identify deeply with the person's situation.

5c When giving a testimony, he/she tends to emphasize the practical application of some verses to his/her life.

9b When presented with a physical or spiritual need, he/she tends to respond best if someone calls and asks him/her to help.

9c When presented with a physical or spiritual need, he/she tends to not respond if the need requires some time for personal preparation.

10b In an organization, he/she prefers to be a follower under another's leadership.

11c When given a task which needs to be done now, he/she tends to favor doing it himself/herself rather than delegating it.

13b If a group is meeting and no assigned leader is there, he/she would tend to let the meeting proceed with no direct leadership.

15b In regard to decision making when the facts are clear, he/she tends to rely on others whom he/she believes are more capable of sorting out the issues in the decision.

17a When called upon to serve, he/she is most naturally motivated to help in situations in which there are specific material needs (food, buildings, equipment, money).

## IX. *Gift of Serving*

3a When faced with counseling another person about problems, he/she tends to identify deeply with the person's situation.

5c When giving a testimony, he/she tends to emphasize the practical application of some verses to his/her life.

9a When presented with a physical or spiritual need, he/she tends to respond on his own initiative to try to meet it if possible.

10a In an organization, he/she prefers to lead a group.

11a When given a task which needs to be done now, he/she tends to leave it for another task if the second one seems more important at the time.

11b When given a task which needs to be done now, he/she tends to be concerned with doing a high quality and thorough job.

11c When given a task which needs to be done now, he/she tends to favor doing it himself/herself rather than delegating it.

13a If a group is meeting and no assigned leader is there, he/she would tend to assume the leadership.

14b His/her reaction to the needs of others tends to be quick, because he/she usually senses what needs to be done.

17a When called upon to serve, he/she is most

naturally motivated to help in situations in
which there are specific material needs (food,
buildings, equipment, money).

**X. Gift of Administration**

1b He/she prefers situations in the church in which
he/she is in a discussion group.

2b If asked to speak, he/she prefers to speak to
small groups.

8c If a person asks him/her to evaluate another's
spiritual condition, he/she would tend to be
critical of areas of that person's life which are
not disciplined and well ordered.

10a In an organization, he/she prefers to lead a
group.

11b When given a task which needs to be done now,
he/she tends to be concerned with doing a high
quality and thorough job.

12a If asked to lead in the church program
somewhere, he/she would tend to choose a
position which involves detailed planning and
decision making for the present.

12b If asked to lead in the church program
somewhere, he/she would tend to choose a
position which involves harmonizing various
viewpoints for a decision.

14c His/her reaction to the needs of others tends to
be deliberate, because of wanting to make sure
he/she has thought it through thoroughly.

16c With regard to financial matters, he/she tends to
feel deeply that such matters should be handled
in an orderly and prudent manner.

17a When called upon to serve, he/she is most
naturally motivated to help in situations in
which there are specific material needs (food,
buildings, equipment, money).

**XI. Gift of Ruling**

1a He/she prefers situations in the church in which
he/she is a speaker.

3b When faced with counseling another person
about problems, he/she tends to give the person
the best biblical solution he/she can think of,
even if not totally confident about the counsel.

8c If a person asks him/her to evaluate another's spiritual condition, he/she would tend to be critical of areas of that person's life which are not disciplined and well ordered.

10a In an organization, he/she prefers to lead a group.

11b When given a task which needs to be done now, he/she tends to be concerned with doing a high quality and thorough job.

12b If asked to lead somewhere in the church program, he/she would tend to choose a position which involves harmonizing various viewpoints for a decision.

13a If a group is meeting and no assigned leader is there, he/she would tend to assume the leadership.

14c His/her reaction to the needs of others tends to be deliberate, because of wanting to make sure he/she has thought it through thoroughly.

16c With regard to financial matters, he/she tends to feel deeply that such matters should be handled in an orderly and prudent manner.

17a When called upon to serve, he/she is most naturally motivated to help in situations in which there are specific material needs (foods, buildings, equipment, money).

## XII. *Gift of Mercy*

1c He/she prefers situations in the church in which he/she is just a listener.

2c If asked to speak, he/she prefers to speak to individuals.

3a When faced with counseling another person about problems, he/she tends to identify deeply with the person's situation.

3b When faced with counseling another person about problems, he/she tends to give the person the best biblical solution he/she can think of, even if not totally confident about the counsel.

5a When giving a testimony, he/she tends to encourage or console others, rather than just share a verse or experience.

10b In an organization, he/she prefers to be a follower under another's leadership.

11c When given a task which needs to be done now, he/she tends to favor doing it himself/herself rather than delegating it.

14b His/her reaction to the needs of others tends to be quick, because he/she usually senses what needs to be done.

15a In regard to decision making when the facts are clear, he/she tends to lack firmness because of people's feelings.

17c When called upon to serve, he/she is most naturally motivated to help in situations in which there are specific emotional needs (fear, anxiety, frustration, moods due to pain and trials, etc.).

### XIII. *Gift of Giving*

3a When faced with counseling another person about problems, he/she tends to identify deeply with the person's situation.

9a When presented with a physical or spiritual need, he/she tends to respond on his/her own initiative to try to meet it if possible.

9d When presented with a physical or spiritual need, he/she tends to respond with money and possessions.

11c When given a task which needs to be done now, he/she tends to favor doing it himself/herself rather than delegating it.

14b His/her reaction to the needs of others tends to be quick, because he/she usually senses what needs to be done.

16a With regard to financial matters, he/she tends to be able to make wise investments and gain wealth.

16b With regard to financial matters, he/she tends to be moved to give generously to people and organizations he/she considers worthy.

16c With regard to financial matters, he/she tends to feel deeply that such matters should be handled in an orderly and prudent manner.

16e With regard to financial matters, he/she tends to work hard to meet legitimate needs.

17a When called upon to serve, he/she is most

naturally motivated to help in situations in which there are specific material needs (food, buildings, equipment, money).